REDEEMED

REDEEMED

The Story of a Marriage Torn
by the Effects of Past Abuse
& Restored by Faith

By

SHANNON M. DEITZ

Redeemed: The Story of a Marriage Torn by the Effects of Past Abuse & Restored by Faith

Copyright © 2016 Hopeful Hearts Ministry
Cover design: Sarah O'Neal, Eve Custom Artwork & Graphics Studio
Printing: BelieversBookServices

ISBN: 978-0-9852503-1-7

Printed in the United States of America

To my husband, Neal,
who often gave 115 percent when it would
have been easier to quit.

I love you.

A NOTE TO SURVIVORS
OF ABUSE

You are not alone. It's why I put every darkest secret of mine out there for the world to scrutinize: because I don't care what the world thinks; I only care that you know you are not alone.

The feelings of unworthiness; of not ever being good enough; of being unlovable, broken, and unfixable (ugh— the fact that everyone who hasn't been abused feels the need to "fix" you); of feeling like you're going mentally insane, pondering if you are schizophrenic because you battle two separate needs and truths—"I want this" and "No, I don't want this"—in the very same breath, with "I don't know what I want" always winning; and of secretly telling yourself that nothing good will ever happen in your life because (see above) . . . well, and does it need a reason? Because any survivor can roll out a list a mile long.

Yeah, I get you. And that's why I know your relationships and marriages suffer. It wasn't until I embraced my worth—I mean, *really* got to the point that I could hold on to the truth that what was done to me was *not my shame* and that *I was worth fighting for*—that I finally embraced the love of God, the love of self, and eventually the love of a man.

INTRODUCTION

In a Hello Kitty journal, I shared my secrets. Tormented at the tender age of eleven, I wrote my first poem to express a truth I wouldn't be able to grasp for decades to come:

Living in a world unknown,
I'm scared to think it could be shown.
In this world I hear voices
Telling me to make choices,
Choices that should never be thought of.
For the rest of my life
I will have to run and hide
From this world unknown.

I am a survivor of abuse. I did not know it when I wrote this poem, yet I was clearly insightful for a fifth grader. I wanted to run from this "world unknown," but instead I listened to the voices of abuse.

Worthlessness was the loudest.

Shame crept in the shadows and whispered reminders that led to insecurity and weakness.

Hurt, pain, and rage shouted out loud in moments when I felt the most out of control, while selfishness, desire, and regret quarreled in the background.

Why did it take twenty years to talk about the abuse? Because it's ugly.

It wasn't until I sat in front of a marriage counselor and heard "I feel like I'm the predator" from my husband, Neal, that I realized how abuse infiltrated my life—*our* life.

God's redeeming grace has set us *free* to love unselfishly and silence the voices of past abuse in our lives. I retell our journey not so others can be voyeurs in our most intimate, and somewhat shameful, moments but to silence the snarling legacy of abuse.

"Do not fear, for I have redeemed you;

I have called you by name: you are mine."

Isaiah 43:1

CHAPTER 1

BE MY PROTECTOR

The LORD God said: It is not good for the man to be alone.

I will make a helper suited to him.

Genesis 2:18

Debonair in his crisp, black tux, freshly shaven face, and piercing blue eyes, my father leaned over and asked, "Are you ready?"

Holding an elegant arrangement of calla lilies in my left hand, I linked my right hand through the crook of Dad's arm and gripped the crisp tuxedo sleeve. I looked at his silver hair and felt ten again, holding his hand as we spent a day being buddies—collecting rent from the college students who lived in the houses he owned near the university, visiting his friend's junkyard, and eating the juiciest hamburger in town. Not really the way a young girl would choose to spend her day, except for the part about spending it with the man she loved most.

"I love you, Dad," I said.

I didn't answer his question. I couldn't. I wasn't certain I was ready, and if I said anything at all, it might be a lie, and I didn't want to start my future out with a lie.

There I stood in the dress my dreams inspired. Pearl white silk, delicate stitching along the hem and mirrored above, along the top of the sleeveless bodice. The cathedral train spread out behind me, the doors to my future ready to open. Yet I trembled.

For once in his life, Dad was at a loss for words. He leaned down to kiss me on the cheek as the wedding march began.

"Ready?" The wedding coordinator nodded at her assistant to help, and they opened the doors wide to reveal 350 expectant faces turned in my direction.

All eyes were on me, but mine focused on Neal. His dark brown hair was perfectly groomed, and I saw a smile start at one corner of his mouth and then spread from ear to ear, lighting up his brown eyes, offering me acceptance and patience despite all my flaws.

This is it. This is for life. Am I ready?

No. The answer came fleetingly, like a minuscule breeze from a butterfly's wings as it fluttered by and out of view. *I love him, and that is all that matters.* I focused on the man who chose to love me regardless of my brokenness and scarred past.

We were meant to be. I knew this from the moment he asked for my number, and I scribbled it on a bar napkin in the crowded club, neon lights blinking and buzzing to life at closing time. He was nothing like the Neanderthal jocks who had taken advantage of me over the past three years. He was a few inches taller than my 5'7" frame; average in height, his lean and muscular body reminded me of Ralph Macchio from the original *Karate Kid* movies. He even had a sense of humor. Earlier in the evening, we danced nose to nose on the cramped dance floor. Gyrating his hips like a Chippendale, he shouted in my ear, "I'm a male dancer!" We laughed and remained side by side as he continued to dance like a newborn fawn trying to find its legs.

The next day he called to ask me out on a date. I hadn't dated in almost a year. I knew I couldn't hide from men forever, and I had tried to accept dates from other men, but the voice of shame from the rape kept me insecure. I doubted a man would be interested in me and accept me for who I was, along with my eighteen-wheeler of loaded baggage. Sharing the details of my past with other men made me uncomfortable, even though what had happened was plastered about the university the year before. Typical of scandal, the flame was quick to ignite but soon died out. I was unsure who would know what, and I didn't have the courage to find out.

On our first date, Neal and I met for an Italian dinner and the movie *So I Married an Axe Murderer*. After the movie, Neal walked me to my apartment and then leaned in to give me a hug instead of the kiss I expected.

"I'll call you later," he said.

And then he left.

Elated and yet confused, I shut the door, wondering if I'd done something wrong. Or perhaps he was one of the first real gentlemen I'd ever met. The only gentleman I knew in high school had passed away tragically in a car accident, and only as I dealt with the magnitude of the loss did I realize the gift Matt was in my life.

My typical experience with men was quite the opposite. They promised love and devotion, and when I wouldn't give them sex, they took it, at times by violent and inhumane means, and left me silenced by a belief in my insignificance and lack of worth. I'd expected nothing more and nothing less from Neal.

My roommates weren't home to sit and ponder with me Neal's every word and behavior, so I got ready for bed. Two seconds after my head hit the pillow, the phone rang.

"Hey." A deep, calm voice came through the line.

My pulse raced. It was Neal.

"Hi," I whispered, not wanting to pierce the darkness in my room with a loud voice.

"I wanted to tell you I had a good time tonight."

For a brief second, I thought I'd imagined what he said. I sat up in the bed and held the phone tighter to my ear. "I had a great time too. Thank you," I said, my voice still a whisper.

Neal talked. He asked me questions about what I was studying at school and about my friends and my family. We stayed on the phone for a few hours, finding out we had more in common than we imagined, coming from separate backgrounds. It wasn't a deep conversation, but it was obvious we didn't want to let the other go. It felt comfortable with him, like a security blanket from long ago.

When we hung up, I thought about all the things left unsaid. Did he know about the rape trial? Did he believe what happened? Memories of the yearlong battle against the star player of the university's football team (also vice president of his fraternity) squelched the safety I felt from our conversation. In a matter of minutes, I listened to the wrong voice. I let in lies and convinced myself I was not worthy of a man like Neal.

I closed my eyes. The healing wound ripped open, and the glimmer of happiness escaped. The moment I had with God I had in college in reconciliation a few months before meeting Neal, brought me back into God's healing fold, but I was still vulnerable to the enemy's attack of unworthiness.

Despite my self-inflicted dose of insecurity, Neal called the next day. It was between semesters, and neither of us had anything to do besides work. I lived in an apartment with three other girls who happened to be out of town for the weekend, and despite my fear of being alone with a man, I asked him to come over for the afternoon and watch a movie.

I was nervous to see him in the light of day. So far we had only seen each other at night. Would my flaws show? Not just the pimple on my chin, but the inner scars that remained scabbed and healing? When I opened the door and saw him standing before me, my nerves tingled.

"Hi," he said and smiled.

I let him in, and my mind immediately went to the negative. *He's not going to like me. What if he's like the others?*

"This is a nice place. We have five guys in our house, and you can't sit on the couch because of the trash." He sat down and looked like he belonged.

I fluttered around the apartment, too nervous to sit next to him, and also unsure where to sit—beside him or on the other couch?

He didn't seem to notice. "What movies do you have?"

The movies were in my death grip. "Oh," I said, my cheeks burning. "We only have drama and, you know, girly movies. Maybe we should go rent one?" I unclenched my fingers from the movies and held them out to him.

"Let's see." He read them out loud. "*Sixteen Candles,* good one. *Breakfast Club,* classic. And *Steel Magnolias,* sad." He looked up at me with a hint of mischief in his eyes. "Eat my shorts . . . what was that? Eat . . . my . . . shorts. Who can pass up *Breakfast Club*?"

We laughed, and my nerves calmed. Once the movie was in the player, I sat beside him on the couch. He held my hand and never made a move for anything other than to eat popcorn or take off his shoes. I was accustomed to seeing the first five minutes of a movie and then battling roaming hands until the credits rolled.

Throughout the movie, we laughed and joked, at times bringing up a memory of a moment when we'd watched the movie before or how the characters related to us or our friends. I didn't want it to end.

"I sometimes forget how funny that movie is," I said. We remained on the couch with our fingers interlocked. "I wish you could stay all day and I didn't have to work."

"What time do you have to go?"

I looked at my watch and panicked. I'd lost track of the time. "In half an hour, and I still need to get ready and go by the store to pick up Band-Aids for the blisters on my heels. I used the last of what we had yesterday. My shoes kill me, and I have to walk the campus all day."

"Let me do that for you." He got off the couch and pulled me up with him. "I'll go to the gas station down the street while you get ready for work."

"Are you sure?" I had never had any man go out of his way to do something as simple as get me bandages.

"Where are your keys?"

"Thank you." I grabbed my keys off the counter and threw them in his direction.

When he returned, he knocked on the door.

"You don't have to knock. It's only me here."

"Well, I wanted to make sure you were decent." He walked past me and put the box of bandages on the kitchen counter. "Oh, and I filled your car up with gas; you were empty. I wasn't sure how far you'd get."

"Really?" I didn't know what to do or say. I was not used to the boys I dated caring for me in this way. I felt my heart grow with admiration.

"Yes, really. It's no big deal. Call me when you get off of work."

We hugged, and he left. No kiss. Just a hug from a gentleman.

Later that night, I called. "We have our last orientation group coming in next week, so we had to get all of their name tags and stuff done. I didn't realize we would be this late."

"It's okay. What are you doing now? Can I come over?"

"Sure." My heart pounded with excitement and anxiety. I wanted to see him again, but what if he expected more from me than I was ready to give?

The second he entered the apartment, I knew my apprehension was foolish.

"It's nice out," he said. He hugged me and headed to the balcony doors. "Let's sit outside."

The balcony was small, with two plastic chairs facing the parking lot. We sat and stared up at the starry sky, talking for hours. Not looking directly at him made it easier to venture into areas that were more private. Turns out we had similar stories to share about our siblings. I'd never met someone else who could share the pain I felt as I watched my sister make destructive choice after choice. Drugs, mainly. Neal knew more than I the pain of watching a loved one squander the gifts and life they'd been given. More so, he knew the pain of loss.

We stared up into the night as Neal talked about his older brother, who had died three years before. Neal was eighteen and had just graduated from high school when Tommy, at twenty-seven, fell forty feet from a highway billboard sign that he was working on, leaving behind a wife and five-year-old son. His mom had been so stricken with grief that Neal gave up his opportunity to play soccer in college to be closer to her.

I looked over at him, my heart filled with the grief I knew all too well. "I'm so sorry."

He looked my way and shrugged his shoulders. "That's life, right? Accidents happen. It's my nephew I worry about." He cleared his throat and looked back to the sky as if for answers.

My heart grew even more for this man beside me. He had suffered the loss of his brother and the loss of his dream.

"Instead of walking on to play soccer for a university," he said, "I took some classes at a junior college and met Nicole."

I froze. *Nicole?*

As if reading my mind, Neal continued. "Nicole is my ex-fiancée."

Fiancée? Not better, but *worse.*

"You were engaged? When did y'all break up?" The hope I had for our relationship deflated. He had been *engaged.* I was probably a stop on the way to their final reunion.

He snorted and shook his head. "We've broken up off and on and now it's been for over a year. He looked at me and grabbed my hand. "Trust me, it's over."

"What?" I smiled to mask my relief. "You can't blame me for asking. So, what made you guys break up?"

"We never got along. I met Nicole after Tommy died. I was mad I lost out on going to college, and at the same time I was worried about my mom. Nicole was a distraction. I did love her," he said, looking at me again and squeezing my hand, "but not anymore."

The voices in my head were loud. Was she prettier than me? Was she smarter? Bet he wished she sat there beside him in my place. We'd only known each other for three days, but I could do nothing to squash the hairy legs of jealousy crawling up my spine.

"Where is Nicole now?" I hoped to sound indifferent.

"She goes to school here. She's the reason I chose this college. Mom got better, and I knew I wanted a four-year degree, so I decided to follow Nicole here, since it's two hours away from home. We dated for a year and then got engaged."

Three words stuck in my head. *We got engaged.* He loved her enough to put a ring on her finger. Feelings like that didn't just go away. Maybe he still loved her. Worse, she could still love him.

He squeezed my hand again. "It's been over almost a year. Ten months, I think."

"Oh," I managed to squeak out and thought about the fact that it was just over ten months since I'd made the decision to turn Zach in for rape. Ten months of taking my self-esteem and giving it a good scrub-down in therapy and group sessions. Ten months of dodging Zach's incessant verbal attacks and threatening phone calls as he stalked my every move. Ten months of connecting with a strength I hadn't felt since I was a young girl and was learning to move forward with confidence. Neal had a broken engagement, and I had had multiple traumas. Ten months of pain for both of us.

"It's over," I heard him say again, breaking through my reverie. "I'm done. I tried to make things work. I love her family and I care about her, but we just don't work together."

I had no reason to be jealous or concerned, when sooner or later I was about to dump my own truckload of baggage on him. Insecurity crept in. Like a snake coiling around a heated furnace, it settled in, content and harmless unless it was provoked.

"What about you?" he asked.

An imaginary vice tightened around my chest. "What about me?"

"Have you had any long-term relationships?"

Only with Matt, and I wasn't ready to discuss that pain, nor could I imagine explaining the relationships I'd had with other men, if they could even be called that—*relationships*. Shame and guilt threatened to keep me quiet.

Neal's smile set me at ease. He walked to the center of the aisle and took my arm from Dad.

Dad playfully slapped him on the cheek.

The pews filled with laughter at the fatherly gesture. Neal and Dad's relationship had always revolved around this type of banter, but it was obvious Dad adored him. He had made it very clear to me early in our relationship he believed Neal to be a man of integrity and honor. Dad felt any man who would defend my honor to an accused rapist who stood six inches above him and outweighed him by at least fifty pounds was worthy of respect.

Neal sealed the deal on his first visit to meet my parents. Bowling was an activity we did as a family, so it was not surprising my parents wanted to take Neal for a game on that first night.

Dad was on edge. We were at the counter renting shoes, and he had his eye on someone sitting in the bar area.

"Who are you looking at?" I asked.

Dad looked at me and with his hand brushed it away in the air. "No one. It's nothing."

Neal raised his eyebrows. I could tell he sensed it too.

We bowled two games, laughing at my gutter balls, and celebrated everyone else's strikes. On our way out, a man walked up to Dad and shoved his shoulder.

"Well, hello, Mr. McGraw."

Immediately Neal left my side and stood next to Dad.

Dad looked pointedly at the much younger man. "Good evening, Mr. Dean."

The man thrust his hand out to Dad. "Don't you want to shake the hand of the man you had fired today?"

"You were given the opportunity to attend the AA classes and keep your job. That was your decision that got you fired."

Dad turned to walk away, and Neal positioned himself between the man and my father.

The man followed us outside, muttering curse words toward my father. Once outside, Neal turned around to face the man, ready to be on the defensive if a threat was made.

"He's all right, Neal," Dad said. "He's not going to hurt anyone. Isn't that right, Mr. Dean? I'd hate to have you thrown in jail."

Mr. Dean held my father's stare with contempt and muttered another curse before turning to go back inside.

"Well, I know you always have my back." Dad slapped Neal on the back and beamed.

Neal proved himself to be loyal and authentic, not full of the trash the other men in my life tried to dish out.

I needed this reassurance because I no longer trusted my instincts with men. On our third date in the first week of having met, Neal walked me to my apartment and leaned in to say good-bye. Naturally, I thought he was going to kiss me, but instead he gave me a hug. A hug. When he pulled away, he stepped back and headed toward his car. "I'll call you, okay?"

I waved in response.

Ten minutes later, the phone rang. I smiled before answering.

"Hey," Neal said, his voice deeper than usual. "I'm sorry I rushed off like that."

"It's okay."

"No, I don't know what's wrong with me. I think I'm afraid."

I sat on the bed, still wearing what I'd worn that night for dinner. I sat up straighter and pulled my knees up to my chest, guarding my heart for the inevitable news that he'd found out about my past and couldn't risk being with me.

I cleared my throat. "Afraid of what?"

The three seconds of silence was excruciating.

"I think I'm falling in love with you."

My eyes narrowed, but my heart soared. "Really?" Could he hear my heart thumping?

"I can't stop thinking about you. I've known you for a few days, and I can't get you out of my mind. I want to be with you all the time, and I'm afraid to kiss you because I don't want you to think that is all I want."

That's when I told him. He needed to know who he was getting involved with, and I was going to give him the key to a gracious good-bye.

"Neal, Zach isn't the only man that raped me," I said when I finished telling him what happened last year. "I was raped in high school two weeks before my seventeenth birthday. I'd known Paul since the sixth grade. It was awful and violent." I shuddered from the memory.

"Son of a . . ."

"I never told anyone until my counselor talked me into telling my parents before I came back to school last year."

I thought about all of the other skeletons in the family closet that were revealed that day and rolled my eyes. He would surely walk away if he knew the magnitude of the drama that surrounded me.

"Are you okay?" he asked.

I smiled and allowed myself to cry then. I could hear the concern in his voice. "I'm okay, I guess. I see a therapist on campus, and I'm in a rape survivor support group."

Then I surprised myself by telling him everything. I told him about Matt, about Paul, and about all the guys after Paul whom I had allowed to use and abuse me because I no longer felt I could say no. I owned their shame when it was not mine to own. Even when I opened the door to let them in, I never asked to be treated with disrespect and a lack of dignity.

Through it all, Neal would utter a sound of frustration or mutter a curse of anger but never disbelief or judgment. He asked questions and let me talk and cry, and even at times made me laugh, for hours into the night.

Before we said our good-byes, he said, "I won't say it because I know it *is* too soon, but I want you to know that I've never met a girl like you before and I really like you."

Was it too soon? The lie that I wasn't good enough for a man like Neal or for the love and sincere intimacy he offered had embedded deeply into my spirit. That lie spoke deep inside, telling me it may be too late.

Neal cradled my arm next to his chest and guided me to the altar. "You look beautiful," he whispered as we took the steps up to stand before the priest.

"So do you," I giggled.

We looked ahead as the priest announced the reason for the celebration. He asked our guests if anyone had any objections. Behind him, above the altar, was the lifeless body of our Lord Jesus Christ, covered in gaping wounds and nailed to a cross. I held my breath and stared at the wounds.

Here I was, my internal wounds exposed, standing next to my bridegroom at the altar. If anyone were to have an objection, it should be Neal.

CHAPTER 2

TO HAVE AND TO HOLD

My lover belongs to me and I to him;

he feeds among the lilies.

Song of Solomon 2:16

Neal, dressed in slacks and a nice oxford shirt, and I, in a fun midnight blue cocktail dress, rushed hand in hand into a sea of floating bubbles as the guests cheered for our marriage and offered their good-byes before watching us leave in a limo.

Tucked inside the limo and on our way for the hour-long trip to the airport, we popped the champagne cork and raised the window that separated us from the driver. Neal kissed me. "Congratulations, Mrs. Deitz," he said. His eyes sparkled, and he kissed me again.

My stomach in knots, I managed a smile. I knew I had tortured him with abstinence for the past eleven months, but I still wasn't ready.

"You want to what?"

We'd been engaged one month. I sat rigid, wringing my hands in my lap. "I want to stop having sex until we are married."

Neal sighed and sat back on the couch. "Well, it's not like we have it all the time now anyway."

"Stop it." When he made snide comments about not getting enough sex, it made the wounds I carried deepen. I wanted to be normal and *desire* sex, especially with Neal, but I felt physically and mentally incapable.

Like a person who suffered a spinal injury that left them paralyzed from the waist down, I was sexually handicapped. One second the person was normal—walking, running, climbing, dancing, enjoying the freedom of mobility—and the next they were strapped in a wheelchair, longing to feel the rough grains of the hardwood floors on the soles of their feet or to feel the throb of a shin splint or to be able to stand face to face with their loved one, kissing their forehead.

They can't go back and make their spine whole again. They can't fix what's broken.

I had been raped. My first sexual encounter, the actual moment of male-to-female penetration, was not joyfully anticipated, longed for, or the result of a heated hormonal embrace. It was forced—ripping, pushing, shoving, yelling, and painful. I felt used and worthless, which led me to be used by others, only given affection and attention for sex. I was forced to do undignified things and was raped by a second man, forced to stay with him out of fear.

What once was whole was now broken and splintered. For years, I tried to wish myself whole again. Normal. I didn't know to embrace the truth that I was spiritually whole and that no matter if I'd given it freely or never offered my virginity at all, Christ my Savior offered redemption, which made me whole again.

Neal reached over, grabbed my hands, and kissed me. "Whatever you need is fine."

The dimmed lights in the limo made it hard to see Neal's face, but I could feel his hands. *This is normal,* I told myself. *This is what you anticipated and have worked on for this entire year in counseling. It is Neal. You love him. He loves you. You are married.*

An internal conflict rose. I battled between the need to show Neal my love and excitement for him and our marriage and my lack of desire to be equally satisfied. The moment triggered a time in my past that had left me used and dirty. I wanted to scream, *Not in the limo!* I didn't want to feel used and dirty on my wedding night, and I knew Neal felt the same, but I couldn't speak.

Instead I went into a detached emotional place I'd created in my mind to feel safe and to hide the ugly. Afterward, Neal wrapped his arms around me and we sipped champagne. I rested my head on his shoulder and blinked back bitter tears as I accepted the truth: this handicap might never be fixed.

Our first year of marriage proved difficult. I traveled four to five days out of the week, working for a men's tailored clothing manufacturer as a customer service rep. Neal's plan to be a high school counselor no longer appealed to him, so he worked odd jobs to help make ends meet. For a short time I was the main provider of rent, car payments, and living expenses that shocked my system and fueled my need to be in control.

A few months into the marriage, finances were tight. The end of the month drew near, and the car payment was due. For two weeks, Neal worked from 11 p.m. to 6 a.m., cleaning out the insides of the tanks at a chemical plant. On the fourteenth day of sleepless nights, he stumbled into the room.

Only the whites of his eyes could be seen through the caked layers of soot, oil, and grime that covered his face and hands.

"I'm so glad that job is over, he said."

He handed me the check for $2,009.59 before slipping into the shower and then crawling into bed. "This should help," he whispered, and fell into a deep sleep.

The extra funds helped make the car payment and left enough for bills in the month ahead. On Monday morning, I deposited most of the check in the bank but received the $9.59 back in cash.

Before heading out on a business trip for the week, I put the cash on the table for Neal.

Later that day, he called me at the hotel.

"What the hell are you thinking?"

"What?" I cradled the cordless receiver between my ear and shoulder and paced around the hotel room. I knew he'd be mad.

"You know what. I gave you a check for over two thousand dollars. I expected you'd give me at least $100, if not more."

"But we needed that to pay bills." I switched the phone to my other ear and stood in front of the full-length mirror on the closet door. I stared at my forehead and the sharp tip of my widow's peak.

"But you're gone for the entire week. You didn't leave me *anything*."

"I did too. I put almost $10 on the table, and there is plenty of food for the week in the kitchen." Sweat trickled down the back of my neck. I walked over to the AC unit.

"Really? You think $10 is going to keep me for the week? I worked my butt off and you gave me $10? Unbelievable."

The line went dead.

"Mom, I don't know if I can do this." I lay on the hotel bed and pondered the fate of my future with Neal. "I think I made a mistake."

Across the line came a stifled laugh. I tensed.

"Shannon, all young couples have troubles in the beginning."

"But not like ours." I pondered if I should say what I felt inside. It wasn't that he hung up on me. My issues were much deeper. "I don't desire him, Mom." I burst into tears.

"What do you mean?"

I got off the bed and went into the bathroom for a tissue. "He wants to have sex all the time, and I don't. I don't want it at all. I mean, I love to be with him, and"—I paused while fresh tears burned the corners of my eyes—"I do love him, but it's not what I thought it would be like now that we're married."

"What did you think it would be like?"

"I don't know. I thought maybe once I was married, I'd like sex more. But I don't. I thought I'd feel more comfortable and not so anxious, but I feel like I'm expected to be a certain way and I'm not."

There was a deep sigh before Mom spoke again. "Have you talked to Neal about this? Is he asking you to do something you don't want to do?"

"No." I blew my nose into the tissue. "He is good to me, but I can tell I don't give him what he needs. Sometimes he makes comments about how we should be having more sex because we're newlyweds and we don't have kids. It's like he's keeping track of how many times we have sex a week, and that is so frustrating."

"Well, maybe you need to find a counselor and start going again. After what you've been through, you're going to have issues with sex. That is a fact. But if you don't talk about it with Neal, he'll never know what it is that's bothering you."

I blew my nose again. "I know."

"You're going to be okay," she said. "Neal is a good man, and he loves you. The first year is the hardest, and you both are going to have to learn to compromise."

I rolled my eyes. "Thanks, Mom."

I knew I didn't have a normal appetite for sex and that Neal deserved to be desired by his wife. The weight of guilt crushed my spirit.

Six months before our wedding day, the priest sat Neal and me down to go over the test we'd taken a few weekends before. It was a simple test that asked us individually about future plans, such as kids, handling finances, and views on faith. There were a few questions testing our responses in certain situations. It was multiple choice and would determine our compatibility.

Fr. Richard greeted us warmly when we came into his office. "Shannon," he said as he gave me a hug, "it's good to see you." He shook Neal's hand. "Neal, you're in here way too often," he joked.

Neal had been in to see Fr. Richard for Catechism instruction. Before we got married, Neal wanted to go through the Rite of Initiation into the Catholic Church. I was honored Neal made this personal decision and would drive three hundred miles every weekend to complete the course to become Catholic before the wedding. Getting married in the church meant a lot to me, but not for the reasons the priest would have liked to hear. I wanted to be married in the church because my grandparents and my parents were both married in the very same church. I was only thinking of the sentimental value, not of the sacramental gift.

"Well." Fr. Richard sat down in his chair and waved for us to do the same in the chairs across from his desk. "Your test results are good. You both are compatible in most of the areas we tested."

Neal and I looked at each other and smiled. He reached over and grabbed my hand.

"However, Shannon," Fr. Richard looked me in the eye. "Your hostility was off the charts." He held up the bar graph score sheet of our results and pointed to a bar that literally went to the top of the page. "You hold a lot of anger and resentment inside, and I'm worried this is going to erupt in your marriage."

I could feel my palm sweat in Neal's hand. I nodded in reply.

Neal's eyes narrowed. "What does that mean?"

Fr. Richard sat back in his chair. "Well, honestly, Neal, if I didn't know the two of you as well as I do, I probably wouldn't recommend you get married until she dealt with some of these issues."

My heart seized. What? Did I hear him correctly? Anger rose through my chest and into my cheeks.

"But," Fr. Richard continued, "Shannon, I know you've gone through a lot over the last few years, and I know you're working on it right now with a counselor. I think you need to continue that work. I also know you two both love each other a great deal. I'm not going to keep you from getting married this summer, but I will tell you right now the day will come when you'll need to attend counseling together."

Neal squeezed my hand. "Sure, absolutely."

I swallowed the lump of anger and frustration that lodged in my throat and nodded.

Lying on the bed in the cold hotel room thousands of miles away from Neal, I thought about that moment with Fr. Richard. We were a few months into our marriage. Was that time now?

CHAPTER 3

WON'T GET ME DOWN

Not only that, but we even boast of our afflictions, knowing that

affliction produces endurance, and endurance, proven character,

and proven character, hope.

Romans 5:3–4

Neal got a job working at an electrical wholesale distributor. He didn't make much, but it had great growth potential and offered a steady income. I worked on my issues with my fourth counselor in five years. The problem was on me, or so I thought. I didn't make Neal go. We weren't *quite* there yet. I held out hope for the miracle therapist who could *fix* me. It took years before I recognized that such a term or any inclination that I was one to be fixed was false. In time, I learned to appreciate my healing journey and the courage it would take to give up relying on others to make me whole and allow God to show me the beauty of who I'd become through my journey.

Once we managed to get through the bumps and hur- dles of the first six months of marriage, despite my obvious issues, we found we still enjoyed one another's company more than we were irritated by the idiosyncrasies.

We were broke, but our friends were, too, which made it easy. Game nights were the rage. One of our favorite games was Compatibility, a game testing the compatibility of you and your spouse or partner. Neal and I always won. On date nights, we held up the five dollars we had to spend and would roll the dice—Taco Bell for dinner or rent a movie? It was during these times we laughed the most, appreciated the small things, and made the most of what we were given.

Traveling an eight-state territory was no longer exciting. Delayed flights left me in a panic. One particular Friday, I was due to fly from Florida in time for game night with friends. The flight was delayed by three hours.

"Three hours?" I wanted to strangle the attendant behind the counter.

"Yes, ma'am. There were issues with the plane. We have to put you on the next scheduled flight."

Like Mount St. Helen, I erupted. "That is unacceptable!" I slapped my hands flat on the table. In reality, I used a few choice words with that statement. "Are you telling me there are no other flights out of here to Houston sooner than that?"

The woman at first appeared shocked and then mad. "Ma'am, I do not work with people that use that kind of language with me."

I can't repeat what I offered in response. With a dramatic turn, I stomped away from the desk and to the phone booth. Cell phones were in use but expensive, and my company didn't pay for the plan.

"Neal," I yelled into the phone loud enough for the entire airport to hear. "My flight is delayed, and I won't get home till probably midnight!" I used my favorite F word. I used it quite often to explain how I felt or what I thought. It rolled off my tongue like poisonous venom.

"Calm down." His voice came across the line like a gentle breeze. "Yelling isn't going to get you anywhere."

Neal could calm me down if it wasn't about us. When I was volatile, he was the direct opposite: easygoing.

"I hate flying," I said. My pulse slowed. "I don't want to do this anymore."

It wasn't only a delayed flight or a change in plans that sent my type-A personality into distress mode. Being alone on the road four days a week was hard to endure. Three hours in an airport was like living in hell.

"Then look for another job," Neal offered.

I stood up straighter, as if he had suggested something unique. "You know what? I am. As soon as we complete this season, I'm going to find something closer to home that pays more and has no traveling."

"Good. Now, get a drink and try to relax."

I didn't want a drink. Instead, I lugged my twenty-five-pound laptop to a wall plug so I could work on my first novel. I bent down to sit cross-legged, and pain shot through my knees. I groaned and rubbed them, straightening out my legs. I hadn't worked out, but it felt I'd done a hundred squats the wrong way.

I dismissed the pain and went to work on *Jailbait*, my first stab at writing a novel from beginning to end. It was a story of a fourteen-year-old girl, Emily, and her first love, Jason, who was eighteen. Her father caught them having sex for the first time and pressed charges of statutory rape. The plot and characters intrigued me, and when I traveled it was nice to escape into their world and forget I was alone in a hotel room or on a germ-infested airport floor.

Weeks passed, and the pain didn't subside. Finding a new job and getting a new car were top priorities. The car would be new to me, at least. During college, I drove whatever car my dad had available. As a hobby, Dad bought wrecked cars and then took them to his high school buddy who owned a body shop to rebuild at a low cost. Often I would get the next car available until Dad was able to sell it.

This time Dad found a brand-new Mazda MX-3 with rear-end damage and a reconditioned title. I jumped at the offer to buy the car, even though we barely had two pennies to rub together. I knew my parents would work on a payment plan we could afford. My parents had not been to La Porte to see our home since we'd been married, so they offered to come down and get us and bring us back to Sherman to pick up the car.

The morning my parents were due in, I took ibuprofen for the pain in my knees. I changed the sheets on the bed and went to lift the mattress when my wrists gave out.

"Ah!" I grabbed my wrists. It felt as if they had broken on the spot. I held my arms out in front of me to examine them. I realized they were swollen because I couldn't see the bone. I looked down at my knees and for the first time realized they were swollen too.

Maybe I got bit by something?

I called Neal.

"When I get home, I'll look you over and see if there is a bite anywhere," he said. "A spider might have gotten you in the butt—it's big enough."

"Ha ha." I didn't care to return the dig.

I noticed it wasn't just my knees and my wrists; when I wiggled my toes, they hurt too. In fact, my entire body was stiff. I'd felt it for a while but realized I was putting it off as soreness from working out or struggling with the suitcase.

What if it was a brown recluse spider? My heart sped up. I had to sit down.

Neal came home from work before my parents arrived and looked me over from the top of my head to the last toe.

"I don't see a bite anywhere. Maybe you're sick." He put his hand on my forehead. "You don't feel hot."

"I feel fine, except I'm stiff, and then if I move my wrists or when I sit down and have to bend my knees, it hurts. Even my toes hurt when I try to wiggle them."

"Your mom and dad will be here in a little bit. We'll see what they think."

Mom and Dad arrived late that afternoon. I was relieved like a little girl, knowing her parents would save the day. My fingers were sore and swollen. Neal had to help pull off my wedding ring.

Mom looked me over and didn't see anything suspicious except for the swollen joints.

"I'll call Dr. Sutherland and see if he can get you in tomorrow afternoon," she said. "He works on Saturdays sometimes."

She made the call to our family doctor, and I had an appointment for 3 p.m. the following day.

A blanket of peace settled my nerves. I hadn't set up new doctors, dentists, or anything medical since we'd been married. I knew Dr. Sutherland, and going back home kept the anxiety at bay.

By evening there was a constant throbbing ache in every joint. I went to bed early but woke up to my own screams from pain that ripped through my gut. I had straightened out my legs, and it felt as if someone had hold of my ankle and had ripped off each leg at the knee.

"What's wrong?" Neal woke up, alarmed.

"Ugh." I couldn't speak. The pain was intense, amplified by every movement. The longer I remained in one position and then tried to move an arm, leg, or even a finger, the pain went from a dull throb to a searing stab.

Neal reached over and rubbed my arm. "Did you take any ibuprofen?"

I nodded in response and wiped my eyes, shocked to feel wet cheeks. I'd been crying in my sleep.

"You'll be okay," he said. "Lie down and try to get some sleep."

After a restless night, I woke up to the same searing pain. I'd grit my teeth with every movement I made to get out of bed to endure the torture. My entire body was puffed up like a swollen Texas tic. I shuffled to the bathroom. My fingers curled up because it hurt too much to straighten them, and I was hunched over at the waist, too afraid to stand up straight because of the pain that came with the effort.

I caught a glimpse of myself in the mirror and winced. Overnight I'd aged fifty years. *Oh, God, what is going on?* I considered praying. I hadn't prayed since Neal and I were married. We rarely went to Mass; instead, we indulged in sleep on Sunday mornings after a long workweek.

I'm being punished. Guilt mingled with the physical pain. I feebly prayed. *You said I was forgiven, but this must be for all that I've done. This sucks. What more could You do to me?*

On the five-hour trip to Sherman, Neal rubbed Bengay cream on my elbows, knees, fingers, and wrists. The pungent fumes nearly burnt off our nostril hairs.

I overheard my parents whisper in the front seat when they thought Neal and I had drifted off in the back.

"I think I had an aunt with RA," Dad said. "She was in a wheelchair most of the time I remember."

Mom looked at me through the rearview mirror. "She says it's in her joints. I don't know what else it could be."

I closed my eyes so they wouldn't know I heard them whispering about my fate. Instead, I thought about all the struggles I'd been through. My fingers curled up in frustration. Stabbing pain shot through my forearm. I turned my head into Neal's chest and cried.

Neal carried our bags up to the bedroom. The pink walls and flowered curtains were what remained of my teenage past. Antique paintings replaced homecoming mums, and the room was crowded with antique armoires my parents had picked up at trade shows, filled with Mom's collectibles. I had spent nights dreaming about my future as a wife and mother in this room. Those dreams never included my husband pushing me around in a wheelchair.

"Try to take a nap," Neal said. "You still have an hour before the appointment."

I stood alone in the middle of the room. The hair on my arms bristled. I didn't feel comfortable being alone anywhere in my parent's home. When I was a freshman in college, I had an encounter with a guy who claimed to have sent spirits there to spy on me.

He was a study partner in my economics class who had a penchant for the occult. One night before our final, we studied at his apartment. He claimed he needed a break and asked if I wanted to do the Ouija board.

"Absolutely not," I said.

I pretended to study but couldn't get my mind off of the terror that triggered too many dark memories of other terrifying moments in my past. The air in the room thickened, and his demeanor changed. I was in danger and feared I was about to be harmed once again. I reached into my memory bank and prayed Our Fathers and Hail Marys fervently.

By the grace of God, it was as if a switch flipped inside his mind.

"Fine. I'll take you home," he said.

The following morning, after the final, I did my best to keep distance between us after class, but he caught up to me and grabbed my elbow.

"You might not want to play with them, but they want to play with you." His eyes were void of life and color, like two lumps of charcoal.

The skin on my neck prickled with recognition. I'd dealt with this evil before when I was young.

"Leave me alone," I said. "Don't call me again."

I jerked my arm from his grasp and didn't look back. I forgot about the threat until a few days later, when I'd made it home for the break and my sister saw an heirloom levitate and fall in midair. The young man called at that exact moment and relayed in detail what we were wearing, where we were standing or sitting, and what had transpired with the heirloom.

It had been four years since that crazy incident. The memory caused my skin to prickle. In trips home over the past four years, I'd also witnessed a TV flying off a table, narrowly missing my feet, lights turning on, and doors opening on their own.

I was crazy. At least, I felt crazy. I never spoke about these happenings to anyone, not even Neal.

Fatigue won over fear. I shuffled over to the bed and forced my aching knees to bend so I could scoot on top. I stared at the ceiling fan as it whooshed in a dizzying circle.

Flashes of dark memories kept my eyes open wide and my heart racing. These moments of fear and evil hadn't crossed my mind since dating Neal. A familiar foreboding itched at the base of my consciousness. I was a little girl when it began.

My flesh crawled with goose bumps. I turned on my side and instinctively prayed, "In the name of Jesus, go away."

I smiled. That's how it started, demanding the enemy to *go away*.

"He wants you, Shannon." The abductor's eyes were pitch-black circles. "He wants to stop you."

"Ah!" I sat up, my heart pounding. For days, weeks, and even months as a little girl, I had heard those words repeated in my head in nightmares. I was eight years old and did not know what it could mean other than that the guy who tried to kidnap me wanted me dead. Now as an adult, it made sense.

We lived in El Paso, where the occult was as common as the Catholic and Baptist churches on the neighborhood corner. As kids, we created a club to get rid of the devil in an abandoned church near the school. We screamed at the top of our lungs, *"In the name of Jesus Christ, go away!"*

The devil became real that afternoon. He was no longer just a character in a Sunday school story. "No!" we heard him respond. Every kid that made up the Mighty Riveras club heard him and felt the fear he longed to instill in our hearts. He was the enemy, and we were his prey.

A few months after the Mighty Riveras confronted the enemy, on the afternoon of my near abduction, I was saved—*literally saved*—by the hand of God. While walking home from a friend's house, a young man grabbed me. He held a knife to my throat and wrapped his arms tightly around my chest as he dragged me between two houses.

A primal scream cut through the air as he shoved me to the ground. The young man took off, and I saw my mother run after him. There was no time to react to the miracle of my mother being there in that moment. She was supposed to have been in a meeting.

That evening, the police informed my parents of the young man's plans to offer me as a sacrifice. It is unclear whether it was for a satanic cult, a possible initiation into a gang, or even as a way to get to my father and his company. One thing is certain: He knew my name. I overheard my parents discussing the unimaginable fact.

Instead of fear and horror of what I'd escaped, I embraced the peace of knowing God existed and He saved me.

The enemy wanted me, if not dead, then crazy. But why? Why did I keep getting knocked down?

In the bedroom, my heart calmed, and the oppressive feeling went away. I looked around the unassuming room and decided maybe the enemy had finally succeeded. I had lost my mind.

Dr. Sutherland's office was empty when we arrived. It was a Saturday afternoon, and the office was most likely ready to close. They called my name, and I shuffled into the patient room. Every toe on both feet ached as I applied pressure to walk, and my knees threatened to buckle beneath me. The nurse looked my way and sat me down in the nearest chair. Pulling a chair up close to mine, she sat down.

"What has brought you in today?"

"Every joint in my body aches. Sometimes it's like a stabbing pain, but most of the time it is a constant deep ache. I can't straighten out my legs or my arms and my fingers."

I held up a hand and showed her my fingers curled into a limp fist.

She reached up and grabbed the hand and with care straightened out the arm. With gentle hands, she uncurled my fingers and looked at my palm and then turned it over to look at my knuckles. When she finished seeing what she needed to see, she laid my hand on my lap and did the same with my other arm and hand.

"When did you have to take off your wedding ring?" she asked.

"Yesterday." Tears welled up. "My fingers were getting so big that it hurt to have the ring on. My husband had to pull it off."

She sighed and looked at me with sympathy. "Well, don't worry. I'm sure the swelling will go down soon and you can put it back on right away."

She laid my left hand down on top of my right and picked up the clipboard to jot down some notes.

Dr. Sutherland came in a few minutes later and did the same inspection; this time, he straightened out my legs, checked my reflexes, and asked more questions.

"Let's get some blood work on you," he said. "In the meantime, I'll prescribe a mild steroid that should help with the swelling and pain."

They took fifteen vials of blood and I didn't pass out. Neal helped me shuffle out of the office, and we headed straight to the pharmacy for the prescription. By Sunday morning, I felt much more like myself. The swelling had subsided, and I could straighten out my limbs without screaming in agony. My pace was still a bit slow and deliberate, but I could pick up one foot and put it in front of the other without shuffling.

We picked up the Mazda, which lifted my spirits, and by the time we were back home, I was able to ignore the constant ache in my limbs and forget about the unknown cause.

One week later, I felt better. The steroids worked, and the constant pain was a minor annoyance. I wore my wedding band again and wanted to forget the incident ever took place. I traveled with my supervisor to Colorado for an event at Foley's, one of our largest accounts.

My boss and I went to use the pay-phone booths by the restrooms to check our messages. The familiar computerized woman announced I had one new message, followed by a beep, and a woman's voice came on the line.

"Hi, Shannon, this is Sylvia Pruit, Dr. Sutherland's nurse. Your blood work is in. If you'll please call the office at your earliest convenience."

I scribbled the number she gave me on a gum wrapper.

My hands shook. I hung up the receiver and stared at it for a few seconds. Erika, my supervisor, looked over and raised her eyebrow in question. She was in the middle of a call with her direct supervisor. I smiled and shook my head to acknowledge all was fine. Was it? If everything was okay, wouldn't the nurse have told me that in the message?

I scoured through my purse and found four quarters to make the long-distance call. The pounding of my heart grew louder in my head as I dialed the number to Dr. Sutherland's office. The receptionist answered on the second ring, and seconds later I was on the line with his nurse, Sylvia.

"Hi, Shannon," she said. "Thank you for calling back. Normally we'd have you come in the office, but since you don't live here, Dr. Sutherland said it best to call you."

"No problem." I kept my voice calm.

"Well, your blood work came back with a high RNA and ANA count, which are the markers for rheumatoid arthritis. He would like you to set up an appointment with a rheumatologist in Houston. Once you make the appointment, let us know and we will fax them your blood work results."

Rheumatoid arthritis? Dad was right.

I was in shock. I was only twenty-three.

Forcing myself to speak, I croaked out a thank-you to the nurse and hung up the phone. I wanted to be calm and act like nothing happened, but the tears flowed regardless.

"Shannon?" Erika hung up with her call. She reached over and pulled me into a hug. "What's wrong?"

"They think I have rheumatoid arthritis," I mumbled into her chest.

"Oh no." Her reaction confirmed my dread. Recovering quickly, she said more loudly, "It could be a misdiagnosis. I'm sure you're all right. You'll be fine."

My hopeless future loomed into view. What was it going to be? A wheelchair at forty? My hands permanently slanted and curled up into fists? Or the agony of the pain driving me mad and making me a lonely spinster because Neal would want to walk away from this foreseeable future?

The news left me dejected, angry, and certain there was no hope for a normal life.

CHAPTER 4

SORROW AND RAGE

Certainly sons are a gift from the Lord,

the fruit of the womb, a reward.

Psalm 127:3

The pungent aroma of eucalyptus and peppermint seeped through the elevator door before it opened. Two steps into Dr. Gordon's waiting room, and the stark reality of what I faced could not be ignored. The decor of the office boasted the revolutionary science of joint replacement: kneecaps and hip bones in lit glass cases. Men and women thirty years my senior sat on the seats of their walkers or held fast to their canes.

Two weeks had passed since I'd received the news in Colorado, but because of a cancellation I was able to get an appointment with an acclaimed rheumatologist. Even the nurse pointed out my luck for getting an appointment so soon.

Luck. Was any of this luck? It was coincidence that I picked Dr. Gordon, one of the top rheumatologists in Houston, who had a cancellation. I filled an empty slot.

Dr. Gordon, an attractive woman in her forties, examined me with the same tenderness as Dr. Sutherland's nurse. She took hold of my hand, flipped it over in her own, examined the knuckles, and then pulled my hand toward her to stretch out my arm. With the edges of her fingertips, she pressed down on different areas of my body and over every joint, stretched them out, and examined the reflexes. She inspected every movable part of my body and asked questions, sometimes asking the same question two or three times.

At first I thought she wasn't paying attention, but then I realized she was testing me to see if I'd give more information or change my answer.

When she asked for the third time about dryness of the mouth, I couldn't keep quiet.

"What are you trying to determine?" I asked.

"There are various diseases associated with a high RNA and ANA count. Rheumatoid arthritis is the most common but masks the signs and symptoms of some more complicated diseases, like Sjögren's and lupus. However, from what you've given me, I think we can rule out Sjögren's, for sure."

She ordered more blood work, and once again I left feeling depleted. I walked briskly past the elderly patients and floating plastic joints to the elevators. The vice in my chest tightened a notch. It felt harder to breathe, and my knees and ankles hurt from walking fast, which increased my anxiety and frustration.

My breathing tapered once I was in the car and behind the wheel. When I tried to press down on the clutch, my legs shook and the dull ache magnified in my ankles and knees. My jaw clenched, and my throat burned with the need to wail as I pushed through the pain and drove out of the parking garage, away from the medical center.

This isn't fair.

My thoughts turned into a day nightmare. I envisioned myself in a wheelchair, sitting by a window, looking out on a beautiful sunlit day but unable to go outside because no one was there to push me.

Neal took the diagnosis in stride, certain we would have long, productive lives together, but I wasn't sure he'd thought about me being an invalid and him having to wipe my bottom.

This sucks.

I punched the car into fifth gear as soon as I hit the on-ramp for the highway. I had a bad habit of conjuring up the most pitiful scenarios. Like movies, they played out in my mind, depicting me as a shriveled-up woman, writhing and moaning in pain with no one there to help.

On a better day, I envisioned Neal pushing me around in a wheelchair. I saw myself as still young but my hands pathetic, twisted limbs curved into fists lying on a blanket over my lap. Neal was in a few of the scenarios, but more often I'd conjure up another woman for him—the sordid affair he'd have because I would be too shriveled up to enjoy life. These thoughts took away from what little sex drive I could muster.

Poor Neal. Double whammy. A wife with no sex drive and certain to become crippled.

It was a miracle I made it home. I ran into the house and flung myself on the bed to indulge in a colossal meltdown. I felt sorry for myself and didn't care.

I was still on the bed when Neal came home an hour later.

"Hey." He got on the bed and rolled me over. "What's wrong?" The worry etched in his face caused fresh new tears to erupt. "Hey now." He leaned down and kissed me, wrapping his arms around me. "Talk to me."

I felt stupid for feeling sorry for myself. I knew it wasn't healthy or something he wanted to hear. I knew it was ridiculous, but the fear had a hold on me, and I couldn't shake it off. I couldn't hold the façade.

"Maybe you should leave me now?" A sob broke through, and I buried my head in his chest.

"What?"

"I'm not a good wife for you," I said. "I don't give you what you need, and now I'm going to be all crippled up before who knows how long. It's better you leave now."

Neal laughed. "You're so dramatic. I'm not going to leave you because you *might* be crippled one day. And I'm not going to find anyone else just because you *think* you aren't good enough for me."

The enemy filled my head with enough lies to demolish my self-esteem. I didn't respond, but I didn't believe him either. I was certain I was no good. For years I had felt like damaged goods because of the rapes, and then I felt freed and renewed after finding my way back into church and going to confession. Here I was, married to a man who was a direct gift from God, but I had taken my sight off of God. I had put all of my worth into Neal and our marriage. Yet the thought plagued me: *What good will I be to Neal?* I was attacked by a disease that could physically cripple my body the way my spirit felt useless.

Like a sinking ship, I was overcome by dark waters of negativity, lack of hope, and unworthiness. I went down fast. It was what I'd known for too long.

I needed to feel in control again. I was desperate to feel as if I had a plan, one I could envision and work toward. A plan that wouldn't leave me feeling useless.

One year into our marriage, I wanted a baby. I was twenty-three, about to be twenty-four, and a baby would take all of my attention and effort. We didn't have money, but we reasoned that if we had kids young, we could be young parents when they graduated high school. By then, maybe we'd have the money to travel, as long as I was physically able.

Dr. Gordon assured me I'd be fine to get pregnant on the medication I was taking for the rheumatoid arthritis. She would work closely with my ob-gyn when the time came.

This meant sex, which was a win-win for Neal. The dark cloud of anxiety and insecurity that hung over me in the bedroom disappeared. Now I was the one who initiated and wanted to make sure this child was created out of love. I felt the desire and longing that had been squashed by the images and feelings that plastered my past.

But the timing was off. I traveled four to five days a week, lifted suitcases in and out of airplane bins, and ran through airports. This exacerbated my RA symptoms, and I was bloated and swollen from the medication. After the first month of trying to conceive, I got my period. I sat in the bathroom and cried. I knew it wouldn't be easy. I felt defeated.

My job search increased, and I found a job as an office assistant for an oil rig drilling manufacturer. It offered a substantial increase in pay, and I was home by six o'clock every evening. Everything fell into place.

I should have been delighted and less stressed, but disappointment hit monthly, as I felt like a failure. To make matters worse, my periods were heavy and long, which didn't leave much time to try for a baby.

Usually this was not an issue for me, but now it felt as if my body continued to betray me. Determined and with my eyes on the goal, I made an appointment with my ob-gyn.

Tests revealed the hormones I had taken since I was seventeen to reduce the heavy menstrual cycles caused the slow release of my ovaries. How was I to know that when the doctor put me on the pill for a cyst on my ovary at seventeen, I would suffer for it later? The same drug that helped prevent an unwanted pregnancy, especially after the rapes, now prevented a wanted pregnancy. It was enough to send me back to church and onto my knees in prayer.

Neal didn't need to be convinced to join me on Sunday mornings. We went to Mass on occasion, but more often than not we slept in and made feeble excuses for missing one of the four Masses offered. Well, I shouldn't say *we* made excuses. Neal never argued about going to Mass. Our attendance rested squarely on my shoulders. If I wanted to go, he went. If I instigated the excuse to let Sunday slip by, he didn't protest.

On the right side of the sanctuary, Neal and I nestled between two families full of children. They played with each other and fumbled with their little toys. The littlest sat on the mommy's lap.

I slid to my knees and cradled my forehead in the palms of my hands. *Father,* I prayed, *I want a baby so badly. I know I haven't been the greatest at keeping up my end and coming to Mass. I know my request seems pointless when I don't ever find the time to pray to You. But I promise You, Lord, I promise if You allow me to have a baby, I will make sure I am in here every Sunday."*

My head was bent so that my hair covered up the tears that stained my cheeks. My heart ached. Who was I to beg and make deals with God? I knew better. I knew God would bless us in time, but I still held on to the lie that maybe this was another punishment for all the bad decisions I'd made in my life. Maybe God didn't think I could be a good mother.

I sat back in the pew. Neal put his arm around me and squeezed my shoulder. "It's going to be okay," he said.

I looked up at Christ nailed on the cross and knew Neal was right, but I couldn't help but think, *Is it?* I wasn't thinking of God's plan for me or His timing. I wanted a baby. I

49

wanted to know I could obtain the goal and be in control. I couldn't trust God's promise, because deep down I was angry. Why did God allow men to rape? Why did He let diseases destroy people's lives and make them anxious about their futures? I was angry because I didn't feel good enough for His love or for a baby.

Years of manifested anger boiled deep inside my spirit, and it changed my personality. The pent-up resentment and frustration caused my mood to fluctuate. My incessantly recurring menstrual cycle compounded the mood swings and left a monthly reminder of my inability to get pregnant.

Neal did everything he could to lift my spirits. To satiate my desire to nurture, he came home with a puppy, a twelve-week-old, crystal-blue-eyed husky named Rocky. Rocky had an uncanny amount of intelligence for a dog and a knack for getting into predicaments. He was the last of the litter. No one wanted him because his snout was swollen twice the size of his face. As a young pup, he'd sniffed out a red anthill, and the ants got the best of him. But he was free, which met our budget.

For a while, Rocky was my baby. He'd sit in my lap and I'd rake my hands through his silky black-and-white fur. He'd lick the tears from my face when I realized it wasn't the month I could surprise Neal with being a daddy. Rocky gave me comfort and purpose. He was a dog to love and loathe.

We'd leave Rocky in the backyard when we went to work or ran errands and would come home to find him missing. We'd search the neighborhood, calling out his name, and he'd bound around the corner, his tongue hanging from the side of his mouth. He'd rush past us, straight into the backyard, as if to say, "Don't worry, I'm here. Where've you been?"

We couldn't figure out how he got out of the backyard. There were no holes dug. The fence we built to keep in our five-year-old golden retriever, Bear, was brand new and intact.

On the many occasions of Rocky's escape, Bear would sit on his hind legs and look at us, look at Rocky, and then back at us, as if to say, "Really? You wanted *this* dog?" If dogs could talk, Bear told us we were fools.

One afternoon, I came home from work, walked into the house, and was assaulted by the strong stench of dog poop. I threw my keys on the counter and turned the corner into the living room, narrowly missing the pile of poop in the middle of the floor. The back window was wide open. I had closed it that morning—at least closed enough to where a dog couldn't squeeze through. It was April, and the weather was nice enough to leave the windows open a sliver, but I knew I hadn't kept it open any wider. Yet the window was open wide, and the screen that was on the window had been removed.

"Rocky!" I looked toward the hallway that led to the living room, expecting him to run into the room. A faint jingle came from outside. Rocky was at the back window, and when I looked at him, he turned his head to the side with a quizzical gesture. The evidence was clear. The chewed screen lay on the ground in the backyard. While we were gone, Rocky had bitten it until it came off, and then he pushed the window up enough to crawl in, then took a dump and went back outside. I would've been impressed if he hadn't left the "gift" inside.

Rocky tried my patience, but he also kept my mind off of the emptiness that plagued me month by month. Eleven months passed, and my ob-gyn prescribed Clomid to increase ovarian production. Two months later, after a year of trying and eight Sundays on my knees begging, I took a pregnancy test and was blessed with two pink lines.

Victory!

I'd endured evenings of torture and pain, refusing to take the steroids for my arthritis flare-ups, and the endurance brought a huge payoff. I never knew joy felt so good.

We had tried for so long, I didn't bother with a drawn-out reveal for Neal. He came in the door, and I practically shoved the pregnancy test in his face. "We're pregnant!"

Grabbing me at the waist, he hoisted me up and then brought me into a bear hug. "That is awesome! Does it mean we have to stop trying?"

I wiggled out of his embrace and punched him in the arm. "Oh, stop."

Nausea kicked in immediately. I hated being sick, but I welcomed the early-morning queasiness and tender breasts. Fatigue hit like a slap in the face, but I pushed through and still made it to work every day.

I was anxious to see Dr. Baker and make sure I did everything I'd heard an expectant mom should do. Over the phone, she congratulated us, put in a prescription for prenatal vitamins, and made my appointment for four weeks from that day. Four weeks? I was stunned. I thought for sure I'd be seen right away. I didn't realize doctors waited until eight to ten weeks of gestation to get an accurate measurement and hear the heartbeat.

Neal and I were on top of the world. I made certain to fulfill my promise to God. The Sunday after I found out I was pregnant, Neal and I went to Sunday morning Mass. This time my hair didn't need to cover shame or tears. *Thank You, Lord, thank You,* I prayed. *Thank You for making our family whole. I'll do the best I can to be a good mom. I promise.*

Neal and I spent every night talking about the baby and potential names for if it were a boy or a girl. We made love without my normal anxieties. We were in love. We embraced our marital vows and our life together. Life was good.

Then one morning as I got ready for work, I noticed dark blood spots on my panties. *Oh God, please, no.* The pounding of my heart bruised my chest. My hands shook as I took off the soiled undergarment. It wasn't a lot, and I'd read spotting happened in the first trimester. This was normal.

Pain pulsated through my chest with each heartbeat. *It'll be fine. The baby will be fine.* The thought of losing the baby tried to push through. *The baby will be fine,* I repeated in my mind and ignored any other thoughts. I put on fresh clothes and got ready for work as if everything was all right.

"There is often spotting in the first trimester." My mind switched back to the article I'd read in *What to Expect When You're Expecting.* I rummaged around what was to be the baby's room for the book my mother-in-law had given me and looked up *spotting*. Once again, I read the article and felt my heartbeat slow enough to stop the pain. The author suggested to call the doctor when this occurred. Relieved, I put the book back on a pile of boxes and went to work.

I called the doctor as soon as their office opened and got an appointment for that afternoon. I couldn't concentrate. I sat at my desk and kept my legs crossed so nothing else would come out. Unable to stay calm, I rushed to the women's restroom. Monica, a zealous Christian co-worker, followed me and sat next to me on the couch in the lounge area.

"Shannon, what's going on?" she asked.

"I think I'm losing my baby!"

The fractured dam on my emotions broke, and I sank into my co-worker's arms.

Without missing a beat, she put her palm on my head and prayed. "Come, Holy Spirit." Her voice bounced off the bathroom tile. "Jesus, heal my sweet Shannon and her precious unborn baby. We pray for Your will in all things, but You've taught to 'ask and you shall receive.' Lord, Shannon wants this baby. Please stop this bleeding right now."

I peeked up at her and saw her eyes squeezed shut and a determined look on her face.

Her voice raised an octave. "In the name of Jesus, I pray this baby is healthy. And I renounce Satan and all of his lies and negative thoughts that he tries to use to bring us down. Lord, we know You love us, and we trust in You. Thank You, Lord. In Jesus's name we pray."

Any other time I would have rolled my eyes and made fun of her charismatic tendencies. But this time was different. My spirit clung to every word she prayed. My only hope was that God listened to her because her Christian life was authentic. Monica was not a hypocrite. Her faith was lived in every moment. She didn't beg God; she asked in His name and within His will. She wasn't like me, who faltered and bounced over both sides of the fence, depending on which one had the illusion of greener pastures.

After she prayed, I was overcome with peace.

"Thank you," I said. I rested my head on her shoulder, and we sat together in silence until I felt strong enough to work.

Neal met me at the doctor's office. "Are you okay?" he asked. His eyes were wide with fear.

I smiled to calm him down, but I could see it would take a tiny heartbeat to accomplish this feat. Before long, Dr. Baker had me on the table, shirt up and jelly on my abdomen. She rubbed the wand around and stared at the screen. Neal and I studied her face intently, but she neither smiled nor frowned.

It felt as if time stopped before she looked at me.

"Well, apparently my machine isn't doing that great today," she said. "I need you to go next door to the hospital, and we'll get you checked out by one of their new machines."

My throat was tight with the effort to hold back tears. "How long will that take?"

She smiled. "Oh, not long. They'll fit you in right away. And then they'll hand you the pictures and report, and you can bring them back here."

Neal looked at me and shrugged his shoulders. He took my hand and helped me off the exam table. In silence we walked hand in hand next door to the Women's Hospital of Texas. There was no wait. I was asked to undress and get on another exam table. I never found out the name of the doctor who inserted a long wand inside of me to get a better view.

Neal's grip on my hand hurt. I watched the woman's face as she punched buttons and took pictures. I looked up at the screen. Neal leaned over me to get a better look. She saw us and, with little discretion, turned the screen away so we couldn't see what she was doing.

I felt the heat from Neal's anger. "What's going on?" he asked.

The doctor cleared her throat. "I'm trying to get a few more pictures before I can make an accurate assessment."

Neal's fury rose, and his grip on my hand tightened. "What's that supposed to mean?"

The pain in my chest returned as my heart pounded. "Neal, chill out," I said. I couldn't handle it. I had a wand stuck up my most private area and my husband about to tackle the ultrasound technician.

She turned the screen back toward us so we could see it clearly. On the screen were two distinct circles, except one looked to be broken at the end and faded into the shadow. The other circle had a little white form inside, like a raisin sitting at the bottom of a balloon.

"You have two embryonic sacs, but only one is viable at this time." She pointed to the complete circle with the raisin at the bottom. And then she pointed to the empty circle that was broken and faded. "This one is being absorbed—or, in other words, it is miscarrying."

Two sacs? One is alive and the other is not? Neal and I stared at the screen in stunned silence.

"You measure to be about ten weeks pregnant. Unfortunately, at this time we are unable to tell you if this embryo"—she pointed to the complete circle—"will continue to be viable."

The pounding in my chest ceased. I couldn't breathe. Will continue to be viable? She doesn't know if my baby will live? I stared at the side of Neal's face. He wouldn't look at me. He stared at the screen with the images frozen in time. We lost a baby?

Like zombies, we walked back to Dr. Baker's office with the pictures of our babies in my hand. I stared at the clear shot of both embryos, the one fading and the one living. How could this be? How will the one living stay alive if the other isn't able to?

Dr. Baker offered no clear answers except to encourage us to focus on the viable pregnancy. She gave me two weeks. Two weeks to lay in bed while my body naturally miscarried the baby. An ultrasound was scheduled at the end of the two-week period. Then we'd know if our baby was viable.

That evening I lay on the couch, chest tight with anxiety, worried about the baby that was alive and dreading the moment I knew was inevitable, when my body would fully reject the dissolving pregnancy.

The phone rang. I was surprised to hear Dr. Gordon's voice on the other end.

"Shannon, I spoke with Dr. Baker and wanted you to know I am very sorry about what you're going through," she said. "I know this is a hard time. She and I discussed at length the medications you've been taking and the general complications RA can have on a pregnancy. I want you to know that we both agree this was not a result from RA or taking steroids. I didn't want you to be concerned this disease would prevent you from having children."

She read my mind. These concerns plagued my thoughts, and she addressed many of them. "Thank you, Dr. Gordon," I said. "It means a lot to know this."

"I know this is an unusual case, and please know I am here for you if you have any questions or need anything at all. You take care of yourself, and do as Dr. Baker tells you to do. I know this baby has a fighting chance."

I put a protective hand on my belly. "Thank you, Dr. Gordon."

Neal paced the room. "What can I do?"

I knew it had to be as hard on him as it was on me. "Nothing. Sit down. You're making me nervous."

By the third evening, he was like a caged mountain lion. "Are you feeling anything? Has anything happened?"

All day I'd felt deep, low cramps in my pelvis. But I didn't want him to hover over me while I lived through the nightmare.

"Why don't you go see what the guys are doing?" I said. "I'll be okay."

"Are you sure? I don't want to leave you alone."

I looked up from the couch and smiled. "I'll be fine. You need to get some air. Besides, you're driving me crazy hovering."

He leaned down and kissed my forehead. "I'll be at Willie's. Call if you need me."

The first contraction hit moments after Neal walked out of the house. I felt my stomach tighten, as if someone squeezed the uterus in their hand between their fingers. The pain shot up my back. I jumped off the couch and ran to the bathroom. I sat on the toilet and stared down at the deep red stain on the maxi pad. Another contraction hit. I didn't know what it felt like to deliver a baby, but the pain matched that of the stories I'd heard—except with each contraction, instead of progress to a beautiful baby, it was torture with clumps of blood clots. My legs shook. I wept. It was over within the hour.

Did I lose them both? Were both my babies gone?

My legs trembled as I tried to stand. I looked down at the crimson bowl and forced myself to forget that a part of me was about to be disposed of by the most heinous means: in the sewer. My hand shook when I touched the lever that flushed the toilet. Neal couldn't see this. I pressed the lever down and stumbled back into the wall. I could still be pregnant. I could still have a viable embryo. I touched my stomach and kept my hand there to protect it. As best I could with one hand, I cleaned myself and crawled into bed.

Neal came home to find me in bed. He climbed onto the bed and lay next to me, bringing me into his embrace. He knew. I didn't have to tell him details.

"Are you okay?" he asked.

I nodded into his chest. My body shook with grief.

It took a few days for the bleeding to slow and then stop. My two-week appointment was a few days away. I stayed in bed and prayed and hoped a baby remained.

In Dr. Baker's office, we stared at the blank ultrasound screen, waiting for the result before it was turned on. Neal had my hand in a death grip, and I couldn't help but hold my breath.

Dr. Baker rubbed the jelly over my stomach, and the screen came to life. There, as big as a grapefruit, was the circle, and inside of it was something the size of a peanut with a small flutter.

"Congratulations," Dr. Baker smiled. "What you see is a very healthy baby and one fine-looking heartbeat."

Our baby had survived.

Neal made a sound like a balloon letting out air. "Thank you, Jesus."

Content to focus on the pregnancy, I pushed the memory of what I'd experienced weeks before into the recesses of my mind. I couldn't relive the moment of seeing a part of me as waste one second more. I had a life inside of me that needed my full attention.

The pregnancy went as expected, with only a hitch or two, such as above-normal rapid weight gain and a surge of hormones that amplified my hostility, anger, and rage. By my seventh month I had gained forty pounds, my nose grew two inches in width, and acne pocked my face, chest, and back. The baby kicked and moved around so much, I couldn't find the right position to sleep. I was miserable.

I was in a state, and everyone around me caught my wrath, including my beloved Rocky. The cute, lovable puppy that left unbelievable but amusing messes was a pain in my side.

Two months before my September due date, Rocky put me and my pregnancy in jeopardy. It was a scorching summer afternoon. I had on a tank top and maternity overalls cut off into shorts. I walked outside to feed the dogs and realized Rocky was nowhere to be found.

"Rocky!" I called.

I heard his bark but couldn't find him. I called his name a few more times and heard him bark in response. I realized he had to be stuck somewhere, so I put on some sandals and waddled around the corner to look for him.

Padlocked to a tree, Rocky had a chain wrapped tightly around his neck, pushing his snout up against the tree trunk. All he could do was let out a bark. With his hind legs, he tried to back away from the tree, but he couldn't get loose.

Fury coursed through my body and unleashed the pent-up rage that waited for such a moment. I marched up to the front door of the neighbor's house and incessantly rang the door bell. The door opened, but the screen door stayed in place to separate me from this rotund middle-aged woman and her grown son, who held a shotgun in his hands.

"What are you doing with my dog?" I was wild with rage, and my face felt like it was on fire. I had no sense of restraint. The shotgun in my face didn't phase me. I forgot I was pregnant. All I knew was an injustice was done and I needed to fight back. Later, the shame came with the memory of living out a moment meant for the *Jerry Springer Show*.

The woman jammed her finger at me and yelled with a deep Texas twang. "Ya dog keeps comin' over her' and diggin' in ma yard. I've called the dog pound, and he is stayin' where he is till tha get her!"

I released a slew of expletives at the woman and her son, and squeezed out, *"That—is—my—dog—and—you—will—give—him—to—me—now!"*

Our exchange would make any Jerry Springer or Maury Povich fan proud. In the end, I stood next to two policemen in her front yard with a ticket in my hand and the dog pound unchaining Rocky from the tree.

I was ashamed. I was not brought up to behave in such a manner, but this shame conflicted with the sweet release of fighting back, taking control, not letting down. It was not the right time, place, or behavior any counselor or psychologist would recommend. What it showed was that Fr. Richard was right. I was a ticking time bomb with hostility off the charts.

Five weeks later, our little baby boy had grown so much that he broke my water and came into this world two and a half weeks early after eighteen hours of strenuous natural labor. I didn't want an epidural. I wanted to be in control of the labor, of everything going on around me, including the pain. My doctors wouldn't let me deliver anywhere but at the hospital because of possible complications with lupus, but I still managed to have a doula (labor coach) to help guide me through the labor pains.

Neal Ryan Deitz II weighed seven pounds, fourteen ounces, and was twenty-one inches long.

CHAPTER 5

LOVE HURTS

Love is patient, love is kind. It is not jealous, [love] is not pompous, it is not inflated, it is not rude, it does not seek its own interests, it is not quick-tempered, it does not brood over injury, it does not rejoice over wrongdoing but rejoices with the truth. It bears all things, believes all things, hopes all things, endures all things.

1 Corinthians 13:4–7

Escape. The first two years of my son's life, I escaped rather than embraced the life I chose. I entered graduate school not so much for the Master's Degree but to have something to do in an effort to feel like an adult. In school I wasn't a mother or a wife. I was an aspiring writer who had intellectual conversations with men who were astronauts for NASA and with retired CEOs of Chevron and with women who had lived through decades of turmoil to come out on top as victors.

I escaped into writing another fiction novel, *Corner of My Mind*, a story loosely based on my own story of rape and betrayal. I joined a writer's guild and attended every writer's conference in the area. Between the classes for the master's program, raising Ryan, and working part-time, I was spent. My patience wore thin for everyone within arm's reach.

In a desperate move to lessen my load, I quit working for the oil company, which drastically reduced our income. I held out hope the move would relieve the stress that caused the irritability and outbursts. Instead, the stress level rose and added more tension to our marriage.

Dreams of becoming an author with the breakaway novel of the year kept me inspired and determined. My novels were going to be a catalyst of change with young adults. I wrote daily while Ryan napped. I sent query letters to dozens of agents for an interest in representation, only to receive rejection after rejection. Persistence and an internal hunch kept me going. I *knew* I had a message to share, but I couldn't figure out a way to release it.

The only person I knew who would understand this inner call was Monica. She had since moved on to another position within the oil company, but we remained friends. Monica, in my eyes, had a direct connection to God, and I needed to know what to do about this longing.

"Just have faith, Shannon," she said. "If God is calling you to it, He will walk you through it."

"What?" I expected her to tell me word for word what to do or say. "What do you *mean*, 'Have faith'?"

"Oh, Shannon, you know." The corners of her eyes pinched when she giggled. "Faith. If you believe this is something you are supposed to be doing, then trust it will happen."

I moaned. She used the T word: *trust*. How do I trust what I'm feeling? How do I trust God? That was the real question.

The nagging feeling coursed through my body and got stronger with each rejection letter. I didn't give up. I kept writing and eventually finished the book, sending out another dozen query letters for agents. Each letter was more creative, and I received some requests for the first few chapters and then the entire manuscript. A sense of hope mingled with the longing to achieve this need, this purpose I couldn't quite describe.

I worked on this writing project with a feverish passion. I put more into writing than I did my son or marriage because I controlled what I wrote and how much effort I put into it. My relationship with Neal faded into the background. We didn't talk; we argued. Both of us wanted approval and appreciation from the other, and neither of us was willing to give it unless we received. So he spent more of his time with friends. I felt both at peace and guilty when he chose to spend time elsewhere.

Ryan suffered the most. I didn't understand him. There were moments I adored Ryan and other moments that left me perplexed and frustrated. I'd play hide and seek, and he'd chuckle from deep within his belly when he found me. I loved his laugh; it burst forth like fireworks and lit up the room. But when he was tired, upset, or angry he'd sit on the couch and bang the back of his head against the back of the couch and hum in a monotone syllable. I'd never seen a toddler with this behavior.

The differences between Ryan and other kids were more obvious when he played with my friend Liz's daughter, Chelsea. She was a few months younger and a few pounds and inches smaller than Ryan. They both loved the water. I'd often set up a blow-up toddler pool in our backyard for them to play and escape the scorching Texas heat.

Chelsea splashed around in the shallow water, crawled on her belly like an alligator, and tried to fill up the plastic water guns to shoot her mom and me but missed and got Ryan. He lunged for Chelsea and tried to hit her with his plastic gun.

"Ryan. Stop." I was on my feet and unclenching his plump fingers from the plastic toy. Chelsea sat in the water and cried. I saw the disapproval on Liz's face when she picked Chelsea up out of the water.

"I'm sorry," I said. My heart sank. This wasn't the first time. He often hit, punched, and bit when a child accidently bumped him or offended him in some way.

Chelsea and Ryan played together often, and for the most part Liz did her best to downplay the situations. "Ryan's a boy. He's going to play rough," she'd say.

I'd feel better until it happened again and again and the disapproving looks replaced the reassurances. Ryan got older and more aggressive. He was a baby, but there were days it felt as if his tantrums were calculated.

"Ryan, you can't go in the garage. It's dangerous." It was nap time, and I needed to get a paper written for class.

"No."

He'd picked up no sooner than most toddlers his age. Not unusual when it's a word you hear often.

I had hold of him by the arm in one hand and a stack of papers in my other. He pulled away from me, but I held firm. "Ryan, it's nap time. You are not allowed to go in the garage."

"No."

He twisted and pulled away, sending me off balance and causing the papers to scatter across the floor.

"Ryan."

I let go of his arm to get the papers in order.

Before I could get the papers in a pile, he had the door to the garage open and one foot in it. I knew I needed safety knobs but figured I had time, since he just started walking a few months before.

His defiance triggered something inside of me. I didn't see a one-year-old exploring, unaware of the dangers before him. I saw a little boy with the mind of a man who did what he wanted to do.

"Ryan, I said no." I picked him up and kicked the garage door behind me.

"No, no, no." Ryan kicked and wiggled in my arms, screaming until his face turned purple. His chubby fists beat on my face.

I took him to his room and put him in his crib. *One, two, three, four* . . . I counted to calm myself down.

"It's nap time," I said.

Ryan stood up and screamed with his mouth wide open and his fists clenched at his sides. No tears. Just the glass-shattering screams.

I shut the door behind me. *Five, six, seven, eight, nine, ten* . . . I counted to twenty and waited for the screams to stop, but his lungs were strong.

He's testing me, I thought. I walked away from the door and went into the kitchen to pick the pile of papers off the floor.

Thump. Thump. Thump. I heard the loud noise coming from Ryan's room.

Defeated, I put the papers on the table and went back to Ryan's room. The screams stopped, but the banging was intense. I cracked open the door to peer inside. Ryan faced the wall. He was on his hands and knees, and I could hear him humming.

Thump.

It startled me. My hands flew to my mouth in surprise. He hit his head against the wall. It was absurd to consider Ryan knew what he was doing or to assume he did it on purpose. I was irrational but not cruel.

Ryan heard the creak of the door and stopped. He sat back on his heels and raised his arms for me to pick him up.

"Oh, Ryan." I picked him up, inspected and kissed his forehead where he'd hit the wall, and settled into the glider to rock him to sleep.

My world spun out of control. Insecurities, fears, triggers, and pride complicated my relationship with Neal, Ryan, and everyone around me. My life was not what I envisioned it should be. I was lost and void of feeling, except for the burning desire to write and have a voice masked by the lives of fictional characters. I finished the first year of graduate school twenty-six years old and miserable.

Early in our marriage, Neal and I promised to start a tradition for our anniversary. I suggested that each year we take turns surprising one another with a weekend getaway to keep the love alive. Neal and I both ignored my depression, and for our third anniversary I went through the motions and made reservations at a bed-and-breakfast in Nacogdoches, Texas, where we had gone to school.

I set myself up for failure. This getaway turned into a reminder of what I wished I could be and longed to *feel*. I couldn't blame Neal, because I was the one who made the reservation for the bed-and-breakfast. I walked into the cozy little cottage, with its white walls and floor-to-ceiling windows with a view of lush green forest, and took in the smell of the fresh lavender filling the vases throughout the room. Immediately my insides turned to stone.

"Check this out." Neal climbed into the pristine white claw-footed bathtub. "Can't wait to try this out." He looked at me and winked. "It definitely is big enough for the both of us."

My heart raced with performance anxiety. The surroundings were too quaint. Too picture perfect. Neal deserved to have a wife that crawled right into the tub without misgivings.

I wanted to say, "It *is* big enough for both of us. Why wait? Let's get started!" But the image put a lump in my throat. *Why can't I be that way with my husband? It shouldn't be hard. We're married.*

The calming sound of a saxophone serenade greeted us when we came back from dinner. The owner had come in to do a turndown service, complete with Kenny G in the CD player, a bottle of chilled wine, and chocolates on the pillows.

Neal shut the door behind us and pulled me into his arms. "That's what I'm talking about."

I love him. I swallowed and tried to shed the unexplained nervousness. On this atypical night, as I lay in my husband's arms, I knew that something special transpired despite my anxieties. For a brief moment, the void and misery were gone, and instead was a taste of happiness.

When we returned from the weekend, life was a bit easier. Laughter filled the house once again, and I was at peace. My cycle, long and heavy, never stopped, but I *knew*. Three months had passed since our anniversary, and my cycle was light. I stood in the bathroom and stared at the sixth pregnancy test I'd taken in three months. *This is crazy. I know I'm pregnant*, I thought. My heart fluttered with anticipation, and finally the pink lines told the truth.

Once again, when I called to schedule my appointment with the ob-gyn, the receptionist set it for a future date, closer to what she presumed to be six weeks gestation. Neal and I walked into the doctor's office clenching each other's hands.

Neither of us said what our minds were screaming: *Please let this baby be alive.* I'd been in and out of the same doctor's office for months when pregnant with Ryan, but this moment brought back the ugly memory in high definition.

Once again, on the table with jelly spread across my stretched stomach, Neal and I stared at the screen with determination. The machine came alive. I blinked, unable to believe what I knew was on the screen.

"Well, what do you know?" Dr. Baker moved the wand around on my stomach and tapped a few keys on the machine. "You've got a baby moving around in there."

"I only see one embryo, right?" Neal leaned over my chest and squinted at the screen.

"Yes." Dr. Baker clicked a few more times, and the screen froze and then came back to life. "Actually, you can see a healthy heartbeat right here." She used a pen to point at the fluttering bean on the screen. "I need to do a few more measurements, but I think we have our dates wrong. You're further along than you anticipated."

I stared at the heart beating on the screen and cried. *My baby is alive.*

"This little guy measures to be eleven weeks," she said, "so that puts you almost out of your first trimester. It looks like your due date will be the beginning of April. We'll have a better date for you at your sixteen-week ultrasound."

Neal and I practically skipped out of the doctor's office. I knew I had been right all along.

"You know what this means, right?" I said to him.

"What?"

"We got pregnant on our anniversary."

He pulled me into him and kissed me. "We should do that more often."

I giggled and pushed him away. "It's all about Kenny G."

One month was all I had between the baby's due date and turning in a thesis for graduation. Deadlines for the thesis, along with pacifying an aggressive two-year-old, threatened to push me over the edge of sanity.

My belly ballooned while Ryan's defiant nature exploded.

"Ryan, sit down so I can get your shoes on, please." I was on my knees on the kitchen floor, wrestling with him to sit down.

"No. Percy. I get Percy." He struggled to get loose so he could go to his bedroom for one of his toy trains.

My fingers got a good grip on his wrist and I pulled him down. "I am late and we need to get your shoes on," I said. I reached for his foot, and he kicked me in the stomach with the other.

I gulped in air. It wasn't the first time he'd landed a kick or two on my pregnant belly. I did everything I could to avoid the attacks, but my belly was too big to protect when I needed to calm his flailing hands and feet.

The attacks felt blatant and full of spite, which triggered a defensive response. I didn't see him as my precious, innocent little boy. The adrenaline from the perceived attack gave me a jolt of energy, and I grabbed both feet with one hand.

"Neal Ryan Deitz."

He fell back and kept wriggling to get free. I turned him over and swat him hard on the bottom three times.

"You do not kick your mommy."

I knew this was not right. As his mother, I needed to be his advocate, the one who raised him up to learn to communicate and react better. He reacted to me, and I was irrational.

He wasn't fazed. "No!"

He kicked his legs, and my grip on his feet got stronger.

"I want Percy."

Sweat trickled down the nape of my neck. "You can get Percy *after* I put your shoes on."

I let go of one foot and struggled to get the shoe over his toes when he kicked my belly with all his strength.

"Argh!" A pain shot through my abdomen, and I let go of his feet.

He shot up and ran to his room. A moment later, he returned with Percy in his hands and a smile on his face.

Ryan and I were on an emotional seesaw. He wasn't always defiant. There were high moments with the deep belly laughs that brought joy to my ears and filled my heart with tenderness and compassion. Deep down, I knew there was something going on with him *and* me, but I was a new mother and couldn't articulate it. Compared to the other children his age, he seemed to be the only one with aggressive tendencies. And I was scared to admit my own behavior.

I felt alone in handling Ryan. Neal would bring a baseball or football home and try to engage Ryan in play, but Ryan would choose to ignore the balls and get on his hands and knees to rock and hum. It was odd behavior, and instead of commiserating with me on what it could be and how we could help him, Neal checked out and went to a friend's.

One rare moment, my mother-in-law witnessed Ryan kicking, screaming, and flailing his arms around. I handled the situation poorly. I picked him up and shoved his thrashing body into his room. I held the door shut so he couldn't escape. When he finally stopped beating his head against the door and fell asleep on the floor, I wiped the tears from my own eyes. I looked at my mother-in-law in defeat.

"How is it I can love this child and not like him at the same time?" I asked. A part of me wanted her to admit what I knew was the truth: I needed help.

"It's just the terrible twos. He's a strong-willed child. It'll pass." She looked at me with pity and walked away.

When I tried to talk to Neal about my frustrations and perceptions, he placed blame on me and my poor parenting skills—the fact that I yelled and was impatient. I couldn't argue with this truth.

The second pregnancy was rough. I struggled in all relationships. It was a battle of wills with Ryan and a battle of pride with Neal. On game nights with friends, the topic often turned to jokes about sex, which ultimately led to comments from Neal about the lack of sex he received. "We don't know what sex is in our house anymore," he'd say. The men would laugh and then complain about how marriage and kids changed the frequency of their sex lives.

Each snide remark I heard from Neal laid a new layer of resentment on the wall I'd built to keep from getting too close. In a thin leatherbound book, I unlocked the anxieties and frustrations that threatened to pull me further into the depths of depression.

I don't love myself, I wrote with brutal honesty. *I hope my future finds me to be a woman who is confident with herself and her abilities, who can look in the mirror and love herself. How can I expect Neal to love me if I don't?*

I slipped and slid into a pit of depression. I needed counseling but I didn't want to go by myself. After the rape in college, I had worked with a therapist for two years. It helped to talk to her about the shame and fear that had me bound up inside. But this time it was my problem to share. Neal needed to go to counseling with me.

"I'm not going to counseling," he said when I brought it up, stomping away from the kitchen like a child.

"Why? Even Fr. Richard said we'd need to go to counseling at some point in our marriage." I followed him into the bedroom.

"Yeah, *you.* You're the one with hostility. Not me."

"But I'm not going just for me. We need to go for *us.*" I sat on the bed and placed a hand on my belly. I wasn't showing yet at the time, but it reminded me why I needed to persist. "We aren't communicating well. All we do is fight."

"*You* fight. I try to walk away, and you *follow* me." He was in the closet, and I could hear him mumble.

"What did you say?"

He poked his head out of the closet. "Nothing."

"No, not nothing. What did you *say*?"

He walked out of the closet and toward the bathroom. "I *said* I'd rather have sex than fight, but that's not happening."

"Why does it *always* have to be about sex?"

He stood in the doorway of the bathroom and looked at me as if I had two heads. "Really? Because you act like it's *wrong* for me to want sex from my wife."

"It's not wrong. I just wish you wouldn't poke me and grab me out of the blue. I don't like it."

"I'm your husband. I should be able to grab your breast when I want to." He shut the door. Subject closed.

My head spun with disbelief. *He doesn't have a right to grab my breast if I don't want him to,* I thought. But the problem was mine; he'd made that clear.

A glimmer of hope came in the mail when I received a "good" rejection for *Corner of My Mind* from an agent. *Make your main character believable and I might give it another look,* the note said.

Believable? The main character was me. This was my story. How could I possibly make it more believable?

Without delay, though, I printed the first chapter for my critique group to review. They had no clue how deeply insecurity ran in my bones. Kicked from all sides, my critique group stomped on the main character. I left the critique session with my head hung like a freshly scolded child.

I give up.

Nevertheless, my desire to write blazed. Once I allowed the wounds of rejection to scab over, I took another look at the blood-soaked chapter, with all of its red-inked dashes, slashes, and scrawled comments, and sat down to rewrite.

I felt like a hollow chocolate bunny I'd find in the Easter basket as a kid. The only thing that held me together was the shell of a person I'd become with a small flame burning within the emptiness.

I want to create a work that will touch people, I wrote in the journal that was a home to these thoughts, feelings, and emotions that rattled around in my emptiness. *I have an urge, a need, to get myself out there in the public eye. But it's not about me. I know from the tip of my heart to the soles of my feet and in the marrow of my bone that I am destined to show people something wonderful, something full of life. What is it? Is it my writing? Will I be speaking? What would I speak about? It's SOMETHING, and it's driving me insane that I'm not there yet. This urgency won't even allow me to write legibly. I get so excited, allowing my thoughts to be carried by this urge, my brain can't keep up with the physical aspect of writing all of my ideas and comments on paper. Do I sound crazy? Someone will end up reading this journal and have to squint to make out what I am trying to write and recognize that I'm crazy. But it's all I have! This feeling. This urge. I wait for the day. I know it's coming.*

If it weren't for the inner call to *do something*, I would've believed I lost my mind. I was lost as a mother and as a wife.

My hormones raged with the second pregnancy, and Neal and I were both sleep deprived, tense, and on edge. Neal worked twelve-hour days. He'd get up early and go into work by 5 a.m. and be home by 5 p.m. Rarely did we have a date night. Early in the pregnancy, choosing to see a psychological thriller movie was probably not the best choice for us to make. After a pleasant dinner, we chose to see the movie *What Lies Beneath*. Neal preferred to see a comedy or a chick flick but relented because I wanted to see a thriller.

Every five minutes, I jumped out of my seat and squealed. Neal's grip tightened on the armrests. I could see the white of his knuckles in the dark. Toward the end of the movie, I let out another heart-stopping scream. Neal leaned over and hissed, "Shut up!"

I bit the inside of my cheek to keep from cursing. We often exchanged harsh words with one another, but he had never told me to shut up before. It hurt my feelings and made me angry. When the lights came on in the theater, I looked over at Neal and could see the lines in his forehead pinched together and his shoulders drawn up to his ears with tension.

Once away from the crowd, Neal started in with a tirade of F bombs. He let it fly like a child with a bad case of Tourette's syndrome.

"I liked it," I said.

"You should've known it was going to be scary. You know I don't like those kind of movies. They make me tense."

Too upset to speak, I let the conversation drop as we headed home, but Neal wouldn't let it go. "Don't go telling your friends what a horrible guy I am and how I hated the movie."

The few friends I have know you better than I do, I thought. I rolled my eyes. "I don't need to, and I don't appreciate you thinking I would go bad-mouth you to our friends. I wouldn't put *you* down."

In a flash, he put his hand up to my face as if to shut me up. Instinctively, I reached over and slapped him. He pulled my hair, and I reached over and pulled his. We had reverted to two petulant kids, resolving the emotions we felt inside by pulling hair.

"That's it." Neal put both hands on the steering wheel. "We're getting a divorce. I need to keep Ryan from being as abusive as you are."

I tensed, and my heart felt like it fell to the bottom of my feet. "But you put your hand in my face first," I said. The tension in my neck shot pains down my back. "Of course I'm going to fight back. I'm not going to sit back and be victimized."

"Oh, come on, I didn't even touch you." He looked in the rearview mirror to see a scratch mark I left on his neck when I tried to pull his hair.

The short ride home felt like an eternity. Caught in the desire to release the deep-seated aggression and anger, I focused on what Neal had done and said. In a feeble attempt to communicate and resolve this awful situation, I wrote the following letter:

Please hear me out. I need to ask you a question, and I need you to be honest when you answer. Had what happened last night—me fighting back—had it been me and a stranger and they put their hand in my face, would you not have told me to fight back? Granted, I'll admit I actually hit you, and I do apologize, but I won't apologize for fighting back. In fact, it has helped me to resolve a fear of mine. For the first time, I didn't sit and take it while I was being pushed around. My instinct was to fight back. Now I know if anyone tries to physically harm me (I'm not saying you were), but if a stranger does, I know I'll have it in me to fight back at least to the death. So I feel the only thing I need to apologize for is pushing you verbally when I should have let it go. But if you think I'm a big threat to Ryan and our unborn child, then by all means do something about it. If you don't love me and want to get a divorce, I won't fight it. I can't make you stay. But I will fight to keep my children.

Neal's words were harsh and unwarranted. Neither of us fought our fights well. I was still a young woman trying to find her worth, pushing to prove no one loved her but at the same time desperate for someone to say, "I love you *still*."

Neal loved me even still.

The next morning, I had cramps and spotted.

CHAPTER 6

CHANGE OF HEART

"Behold, I stand at the door and knock. If anyone hears my voice

and opens the door, [then] I will enter his house and

dine with him, and he with me."

Revelation 3:20

Without suffering, you would not know joy. There was no greater joy than the ultrasound screen coming to life and my little boy moving about and noticeably sucking his thumb. The spotting was residual from my cycle that continued even into the first trimester of pregnancy.

This scare of losing another baby was all I needed to kick into gear an internal longing to find faith. Something had to give. Losing Ryan's twin was devastating and difficult, and it led me back into church, but I didn't know where I stood with God except to know I didn't want to give myself entirely to Him. I wanted to remain in control and make decisions with my own free will. I'd shied away from becoming what I felt was a "Jesus Freak" because I didn't want to be that person who appeared perfect but judged others because they made a mistake or two.

First, I made a New Year's resolution to read the entire Bible in a year. My best friend gave me a Bible in middle school, but it was not used.

Second, I set out to determine what I needed to change in order to become a better mother and wife. Every morning I looked in the mirror, I knew this resolution could be the most daunting. I had a lot to change.

Third, I resolved to remain true to the overwhelming desire to do something that would help others.

In the first month of January 2001, when I was seven months pregnant, a friend asked me to attend a Bible study called "Breaking Free" by Beth Moore at the local First Baptist Church.

"We meet once a week in someone's home," she said, "but they offer free babysitting at the church."

Free babysitting? Breaking free? I was one of the first to sign up. Seven months pregnant and carting a defiant and restless two-year-old into the church building, I prayed they wouldn't call me away from the study for his bad behavior.

Nestled in the softest cowhide leather recliner in the room, I let out a pleased sigh. Quiet. This was the breaking free I needed.

The room filled with women of all ages. We went around the room, introduced ourselves, and expressed our motives for taking the study.

I surprised myself by saying, "I'm lost in my faith. I'm hoping this study will help me find my way back."

I expected smirks and knowing looks, the judgment of perfect people. But there were many nods and looks of understanding. Others chimed in and admitted they weren't where they felt they needed to be in their relationship with God.

I listened intently as the rest of the ladies went through their introductions. Normally I would politely excuse myself when others spoke of God and being in relationship with Him, but I was intrigued. After introductions, we turned our attention to the television screen for the introductory message from Beth Moore, and I realized this wouldn't be a few hours of simple girl talk.

I took the workbook home with less apprehension than when I received it and flipped through the 220 pages of material and questions. I read through Day 1, and my breath caught. It discussed Uzziah from 2 Chronicles 26:1–23 and what he was able to do with God's strength and how pride was his downfall. The word *pride* rattled my spirit, and I continued on through the week with the daily study, learning more and more about pride and the blessings it keeps from us. I learned that much of our own captivity is caused by a failure to remove the obstacles of unbelief, pride, idolatry, prayerlessness, and Spirit-quenching legalism, yet God still woos us to a spacious place free of earthly bonds.[1]

The lesson resonated with me. Every obstacle mentioned touched me on different levels. *Unbelief*—did I be-

---

1   Beth Moore, *Breaking Free Bible Study: Making Liberty in Christ a Reality in Life* (Nashville: LifeWay, 1999), pg.11.

lieve in God's promise to take care of me, to be my protector and love me despite the sin that remained from the years past? *Pride*—would I be able to overcome the perception I had of those who were "Jesus Freaks"? To me, they were self-righteous goody-goodies who judged as they preached. Worse, would I be able to truthfully admit to my own faults? *Idolatry*—did praying to Mary count? Or was being Catholic an instant sin of idolatry?

This confused me even more. I recalled lessons from my middle school youth minister, who happened to be with another Christian denomination outside of my home Catholic parish. His lack of tact and direct judgment toward Catholics, essentially me, caused me to walk away from my faith. The memory added an edge of doubt to my recent pursuit of what I'd given up.

Prayerlessness—I cringed. As a young girl, I prayed fervently to God, but I'd stopped because I felt my prayers were hitting brick walls. Only when I wanted something— like a child—did I consider prayer. Like the promise I made to God when I begged him to get pregnant with Ryan. The shame made my throat tighten. *Spirit-quenching legalism*—I was lost. I had to find out.

The following week, I settled into the same leather recliner and laid the book across my lap, ready to dig into the discussion. We went about the room, taking turns reading the questions and giving the answers. When we came to Day 5 and the particular paragraph that stated the obstacles that keep us from God, one of the ladies shot her hand up in the air.

"What is legalism?" she asked.

My heartbeat soared with relief at not having to ask the very same question and realizing that someone else didn't know. I wasn't alone in my ignorance.

The facilitator didn't skip a beat. "It is when you are really strict to the Law. Like the Pharisees, when they were upset with Jesus because He taught in the synagogue on the Sabbath."

Another woman who sat across from me spoke up. "Isn't it also making your faith more about the tradition than the relationship with Christ? You know, like Catholics?"

My heart pounded in my chest at the mention of Catholics, and I could feel the blood rise to my cheeks. The only person who knew I was Catholic was the girlfriend who had invited me to the study. She looked over at me with wide eyes.

Someone else piped up. "Yeah, I went to a Catholic church one time. It was a bunch of sitting and standing. I had no idea what was going on. And they have all of those statues in the church. That's idolatry, too, isn't it?"

I was certain they could hear the pounding of my heart. I wanted to come to the Catholic Church's defense but was frozen by a lack of knowledge. I knew the Catholic faith wasn't as cut and dry and mechanical as they were making it out to be, and we didn't sit around worshiping statues.

The facilitator cleared her throat before answering. "Well, I can't say for sure because I'm not Catholic and I don't know about the faith. I know they pray to Mary, and we are taught you should only pray to God."

"Well, Shannon's Catholic," my friend spoke up and pointed at me. "Shannon, do you know anything about this?"

For a brief second I wished I had the power of laser beams to shoot from my eyes and zap my friend into a pile of ashes. *What are you doing to me?* I raged inside. Every pair of eyes in the room was on me.

"There is more to Mass than sitting and standing," I said. I groped for the words that would help me sound as if I knew what I was talking about. "I know our entire Mass comes from the Bible, and we don't sit around praying to statues."

"But you pray to Mary?"

"Yes." I hesitated. "Well, kind of. I mean we pray to her to pray *for* us. We don't pray to her like we pray to God. You know, it's like praying to your grandmother in heaven, asking her to pray for you."

I knew there had to be a better answer, but I was forced to recognize my ignorance about my own faith. Defeated, I squirmed in the chair.

Some of the women discussed this concept of praying to our deceased loved ones.

I decided to be honest. "You know," I said, loud enough for everyone to hear, "I'm not sure of a lot of things about my Catholic faith, but I guess that's why I'm here. I want to know more about faith in general, and then I'll figure out where I belong."

When the study was over, I recognized the mistake I made in the announcement. One lady after another invited me to their church services and to join them for adult church activities. It was nice to be welcomed but overwhelming at the same time. It wasn't that I needed to belong. If I was going to be honest with myself, I wasn't there to have a child-free morning of quiet. I wanted to feel God in my life again.

I struggled with a desire to give up the study and not go back to the small group. I didn't like being the only Catholic, even if I wasn't sure I wanted to remain Catholic. It made me uncomfortable for them to bring up the Catholic Church as if it was a bad entity.

God knew I needed the push to continue, as in the last paragraph of Day 5 of that week, Beth wrote:

Anyone who is taking this study for the pure satisfaction of completing another Bible study won't stay interested long. . . . This Bible study is for the heart—to loosen any chains withholding the heart from enjoying the abundant liberty in Christ's salvation. If we let our mouths grow close to him through churchy conversation and even theological discussion in small groups, but we keep our hearts far from Him, this journey will not mean a thing. For indeed, we never left "go".[2]

That's all I needed to hear. I underlined the section, highlighted it, and circled it. If any more talk of the Catholic Church came up, I would go back to this section and read aloud.

Weeks went by. I got bigger (or the chair got smaller), and the Bible study went deeper and deeper, reaching the depths of my spirit, where I hid hurts, lies, and untruths

---

2   Ibid., pg. 70.

under lock and key. Key phrases leapt off the pages, such as "Shame is Satan's 'stamp of approval'" and "An unhappy woman usually needs a change of heart more than of circumstances." These words resonated from week to week, along with the promises I read in the Bible every night as I pored over the Psalms, Proverbs, and Isaiah. All of these words, phrases, and stories had meaning to me in my present moment. I'd heard the same psalm read at Mass or had even read a passage from the Old Testament when I was a lector, but it bounced off of me instead of sticking.

Toward the end of the study and the end of my pregnancy, we focused on the path to freedom. The study asked, "Do you also have authority problems? If so, how have you become aware of them?"

I have a problem with control, I wrote. *I don't want to be controlled in any way. Not by man or God.* Revealing this truth and seeing it revealed in black ink added a fresh new layer of pain to the thick coat that protected my heart. The study spoke of a freedom I longed for—to be free from the oppressive shield, but it was comfortable and the only security I could hold on to.

Resolved to be transparent in my answers, I wrote out a prayer to God: *Jesus, take away the heavy burden of guilt I've managed to wrap myself in, and let's walk together to finish my story.*

My issues with control were deep. I had chosen natural childbirth when I delivered Ryan because I didn't want to lose control with the drugs that were given. I wanted to feel my legs and be in control of the pain as much as I physically could handle.

This pregnancy was no different. My water broke a week before I was due to deliver. I thought I was prepared to suffer through the pain as I had with Ryan, but this delivery was different. The contractions were harder and faster than I remembered. They came in waves that crashed over me and threatened to knock me down mentally, physically, and emotionally. This was not a pain like being cut or falling and scraping your leg. It was a sensation that rose up from inside that was so foreign and uncomfortable, it made every part of my mind and body recoil from its atrocity.

Laid out on the bed, legs splayed and body demanding to push, the waves of pain became so intense I couldn't help but let out a deep snarling growl that rose into an ear-piercing scream.

The labor nurses whispered to one another. "She's going to scare the other women on the floor."

I didn't care who I scared. All I cared about was making it stop.

Neal, my mom, and my doula, Heidi, were at my side, along with Liz, who filmed the birth. It was a crowded room, but it didn't matter because I couldn't get past the pain that felt as if it was tearing my body apart.

Neal grabbed my hand. "Just breathe. You'll be okay. Just breathe."

A second wave crashed, and it felt so unbearable that I wanted to let go of reality and ride it into darkness. As the thought came, I pictured Christ standing before me. He picked me up and cradled my limp body in His arms.

"I have you," He said.

"Jesus."

The pain was intense, but it was as if Jesus's body absorbed enough so I could manage.

The doctor rushed in. "Push!" she said.

On cue, my body sprang into action, and I pushed as hard as I could.

After a few long hard pushes, I could hear the doctor and nurses talking in whispers, and then one of the nurses stood over me.

"Your cervix didn't thin," she said. "We need to reach in and pull it over his head."

I didn't have time to acknowledge what she said. The doctor reached in, and it felt as if she tore my uterus out with her bare hands. My son's shoulders were also too wide, so at the same time they pulled the cervix over his head, they twisted his body and pulled him out. The scream that escaped my lips will undoubtedly forever be burned in every person's memory present that day.

The gift in the pain was that as soon as it came, it was also gone. In a matter of seconds, I held my precious newborn son, Seth Thomas Deitz.

A quiver coursed through my body as it went back to its natural form, and tears of joy and relief ran down my face, landing on my wailing nine-pound boy. The void, the failure, the shame—it all went away in this brief taste of pure joy.

But there was no time to waste once Seth was born. I still had four weeks to complete my thesis novel and deliver it to the committee before graduating. And I didn't want to miss out on the last week of Bible study.

With Seth in my arms, I sank carefully into the worn leather seat that had been mine every Wednesday for the past three months. I read through the week with everyone, getting to hear the words of wisdom for the first time because I clearly didn't have time to do the study on my own.

One of the paragraphs made my heart skip a beat:

Go where He goes and let Him fight for you. Invariably when we're most exhausted, we'll find we're expending more energy fighting the enemy than we are seeking God's presence. More than you seek to win, seek Christ! More than you seek to defeat the enemy, seek his foe! More than you seek victory, seek the Victor! As you do, you are binding yourself to His presence and <u>trusting God to carry you</u> onto victory.[3]

Just as He had carried me through labor.

There was no denying it anymore. God sought after me, and it both enticed and scared me to death. I wasn't sure if I was ready for where God wanted to take me spiritually. Like a child, I hid behind my mother's skirt, grasping

---

3   Ibid., pg. 219.

the comfort of the control, but peeked around at the loving God who beckoned with His forgiveness and love.

At the table with an intimidating group of professors who had read through my thesis, *Crossroad Collision*, I felt the first stirrings of something greater than failure, guilt, and shame.

"You're a great writer," one of them said.

I didn't expect to hear praise, especially after receiving rejection after rejection over the past few months.

The other professors agreed. They offered useful, constructive criticism that made me feel like I'd dipped my hand into a pot of gold because I knew how valuable what they revealed would mean to my craft. It solidified the insistent desire that I would someday use writing for the good.

I had purpose and worth.

CHAPTER 7
A TASTE OF HEAVEN

That you should put away the old self of your former way of life,

corrupted through deceitful desires, and be renewed in the spirit

of your minds, and put on the new self, created in God's way in

righteousness and holiness of truth.

Ephesians 4:22–24

Graduation was over. The Bible study was over. All that was left was my life as mother and wife, and for the first few weeks it was glorious. Invigorated with purpose, I felt like I was given a rope to pull me from the raging waters of insecurity, unworthiness, and pride.

Seth was a good baby. He nursed well, he slept well, and he was calm. The only problem was trying to wrestle with Ryan and his pent-up energy and aggression.

On more than one occasion when I nursed Seth, Ryan came over and wanted attention too. I knew it was normal for a toddler. I didn't mind. What troubled me was when he jumped on top of the both of us to get attention. He'd miss Seth's fragile skull by inches with his knee. I'd scold him and at times reflexively push him away in order to save Seth from the impending crush. Ryan would fall to the ground, wail, and then bang his head on the wall or lie there and kick and scream until I put Seth down to offer him the attention he craved.

I assumed what bothered Ryan the most was the fact that I held Seth close when I fed him. When I tried to hold Ryan, he arched his back and pulled away, as if my touch burned. Defeated, I backed away with a wounded heart. It solidified that I was not a good mother. I couldn't find a way to love him.

One night Ryan and I reached our pinnacle. Neal had escaped with his friends, and I was alone with the kids. Like clockwork, Seth was ready to feed, so I checked in on Ryan, who was playing with trains in his room. *Thomas the Train* played on the little television, so I settled in the living room with Seth for what I expected to be an uninterrupted feeding.

Ten to fifteen minutes went by, and I realized the house was blissfully quiet. Too quiet. I heard the sound of the video coming from Ryan's room, but I couldn't hear Ryan talking as he often did to the trains or making choo-choo noises. The thought crossed my mind there might be an issue.

I smelled it before I could see it.

Ryan came around the chair with his hands held out in front of him like Frankenstein, fingers spread like fans. His fingers, hands, and wrists were caked in poop, as if he'd been crafting a pottery bowl.

Disgusted, I jumped out of the chair, which jarred Seth and stopped his feeding.

Ryan looked up at me, and his eyes got wide. I ran past him and put an unhappy, wailing Seth in his crib. The trail of poop droppings led down the hall to the bathroom. Close behind, Ryan walked stiff-legged, with no pants or underwear.

He was potty-trained, but we had issues with going number two. It was obvious he tried to do it on his own. A low squeal escaped when I saw what appeared to be a toxic waste explosion in the bathroom. Poop was everywhere. Little handprints smeared along the shower curtain, swiped across the tile floor, and ran along the base and seat of the toilet. He had also tried to wipe himself, because half the roll of soiled toilet paper was bunched up around the base on the floor.

Why are you doing this to me? What have I done to you to deserve this? These selfish thoughts stormed in my head. I felt controlled and, at the same time, *out* of control, which triggered an irrational response. Out of the corner of my eye, I saw Ryan's soiled underwear and grabbed it. With pure disgust and anger, I turned to him to shove the underwear in his face.

A firm pressure, like a hand on my arm, stopped me. Ryan's big blue eyes stared at me with fear. My breath caught. I finally saw my child.

My child.

My flesh.

My blood.

My eyes.

My nose.

My love.

My child.

I dropped the underwear. Shame. Pure shame gutted me, and I cried out in pain. I reached for my precious son and drew him into my embrace. "I'm sorry, Ryan. Let's get you cleaned up."

I took him gently by the hand and cleaned him up with a wet washcloth. In the background, I could hear Seth's wails, but I focused on the child in front of me.

"Jesus, help me. Jesus, help me. Jesus, help me," I prayed.

I cleaned Ryan up, put him in the tub, and went to check on my wailing baby.

I gasped at the sight of smeared spit-up all over Seth's pinched face. His little hands were in tight fists, and with each wail he flailed them around, smearing the spit-up across his face.

"Oh my God!" I cried.

In a panic, I grabbed Seth from the crib and used my shirt to wipe the spit-up off his face.

I moved on autopilot, driven by shock and shame. I was ashamed of myself and angry at Neal for not being with me to help. He spent more and more time with friends. In this moment, I had never felt more alone.

With Seth in my arms, I rushed back to Ryan, who was blissfully happy playing in the tub. I turned the water off and grabbed a new washcloth from the cabinet and wet it to wash off Seth's face and hands. His wails subsided into a whimper. I knew he was still hungry, but I needed to get Ryan cleaned and out of the tub.

"Jesus, help me. Jesus, help me," I kept praying. Saying those three words calmed me enough to move one step at a time. I managed to find a pacifier to soothe Seth and placed him in a bouncy seat at my feet while I washed Ryan off. The stench in the room made my eyes water. I was careful not to get near the toilet or touch the part of the shower curtain that was soiled.

Within minutes, I had Ryan bathed, dressed, and safely in his room watching a *Thomas the Train* movie. Shame and guilt orchestrated my behavior, so I stayed with him in his room. I sat on his big-boy bed and nursed Seth. Ryan crawled up on the bed beside me, and for the first time since Seth was born, he lay still by my side without trying to push Seth off or punch him in the face. I rubbed his back with my free hand.

The shock wore off. I felt the heat of tears as they soiled my face. Thomas the Train tooted his whistle on the screen, but my eyes glazed over as I recalled the rage and anger that welled up inside me in that dreadful moment.

Seth finished eating, and mechanically I burped him. He fell asleep with his head resting in the crook of my neck. I blinked and realized the credits were on the television screen, but Ryan wasn't throwing his normal fit to have another tape put in. I looked down beside me.

Ryan's eyes were closed and his little mouth open. His face was so peaceful. I looked at both of my babies and realized how vulnerable they were. I leaned down and kissed

Ryan's forehead, scooted off the bed so as not to wake him, and went to Seth's room and laid him gently in his crib.

The stench of Ryan's creativity filled the hallway. With lead feet I turned toward the kitchen for the cleaning supplies and headed back into the bathroom to finish the job. With each scrub, wipe, and rinse, I sobbed harder and harder, "Jesus, help me." I kept the mantra going. I couldn't think of any other words to say that would break apart the boulder of stone that filled my chest.

The bathroom clean and a second check of the boys done to make sure they were still asleep, I headed to the sanctity of my bedroom. I sat down on the edge of my bed, defeated. I hadn't felt this low since the day I walked away from Paul's house, only sixteen years old and no longer a virgin, certain any redeeming quality about me had been beaten and torn away in the struggle that had ensued in his bedroom.

I thought I had overcome all those years of living in deep despair, depression, and regret. I thought I had worked my way back into God's good graces. I went to confession, and Neal came into my life and accepted me, even though I was demanding and hard to please. But the years passed, and I hadn't been to confession since. My church attendance was sporadic, even after the promise I made to God when I was pregnant with Ryan. My emotions jumbled like a ball of thread, and I wasn't sure what I felt about my marriage, my faith, or my life.

The Bible study workbook on the nightstand, ready to be thrown away, caught my eye. I leaned over, picked it up, flipped through the pages, and came to rest on page 121, where I had underlined, "No matter what has happened to us, what we have done, or where we have been, you and I are brides! It's high time we see ourselves as we really are."[4]

I shook my head in response to the same sentence I had wanted to claim only months before. I wanted to feel like Christ's bride. I wanted to feel worthy of His love and approval. I didn't want to be this person I had become—angry, bitter, resentful, frustrated, undone, and unhappy.

The page crinkled and curled from the tears that fell and blurred my vision. I flipped through again and stopped only to wipe my eyes and nose with the back of my hand. I looked down at page 119 and read what I had underlined: "If Satan has convinced you to see yourself as anything less than the handpicked daughter of the King of all kings, you have something in common with Tamar. . . . What you may have in common is a stronghold. My prayer is that the Holy Spirit will be free to mend the torn coats of the daughters of royalty. And that he will also restore lost dignity, teach us our true identity, and liberate us in purity."[5]

I had underlined *purity* three times. And in the corner of the page, I read my handwritten prayer: *Lord, help me mend my torn clothes! Take that wall away that is blocking me from seeing how I am beautiful and pure in Your kingdom. Heal my wounds and let me live.*

I whimpered and wiped my eyes. *I want to live*, I thought.

---

4   Beth Moore, *Breaking Free*, 121.
5   Ibid., 119.

101

I flipped through the book as if God was going to jump out from the pages, grab me, and suck me into a more pleasant world. I went back to the beginning of the book, on page 45, and read:

What does it take? Paying attention to God's commands (by obedience) through the power of the Holy Spirit within us? Why should we? Because God is incapable of making mistakes with our lives. Isaiah 48:17 tells us He teaches us only what is best for us. He directs us only in the way we should go. Obedience to God's authority not only brings peace like a river but righteousness like the waves of the sea. Not righteous perfection. Righteous consistency.[6]

Gravity pulled me to the ground, and I fell to my knees. *I can't do this anymore.* Sobs shook my entire body. Desperate to end the pain, I lay flat on the floor with my face in the matted, dingy carpet. Everything I had done in the past four years that was impure, nasty, rude, mean, done out of anger, and hateful toward others or myself rushed through my mind and pushed the sobs forward, rattling every bone in my body. In the confines of my mind, I screamed. *I don't want to be this person anymore! I don't want to live this life anymore! I don't want to be here!*

Beth Moore's words pushed through the noise in my head: "What does it take? Paying attention to God's com-

---

6   Ibid., 45.

mands through the power of the Holy Spirit within us. . . . My prayer is that the Holy Spirit will be free to mend the torn coats of the daughters of royalty."

My defiant nature took over, and I stopped in midcry. With clenched fists, I pushed myself up to my knees and prayed, *Holy Spirit, if You are in me, then do something with my life! I don't want to be this person anymore. I'm done. Holy Spirit, help me.*

In a simple breath, I felt peace wrap around my shoulders like a warm blanket and the weight of the boulder in my chest disappeared, replaced by an explosive energy that coursed through my body and made me smile through the tears. For a brief moment, I felt a love that I'd known when I was a child. A love that is certain and uncontested. A love with no conditions or judgment. I smelled His purity and grace. It was a taste of heaven.

I sat back on my heels and cried tears of joy. I had found God again. The God I knew as a young girl. The God I thought I disappointed and whose perfection I thought I could never live up to. In that moment, I knew all I wanted was to be with Him. To do whatever it meant to make sure I could feel His peace wrap around me for eternity. I knew I was forgiven and redeemed.

Spent, I got up off the floor, put the workbook back on the nightstand, crawled into bed, and fell into a deep sleep.

CHAPTER 8

ONE DAY AT A TIME

Trust in the LORD *with all of your heart, on your own*

intelligence do not rely; in all your ways be mindful of him,

and he will make straight your paths.

Proverbs 3:5–6

Life was not perfect because I had found God or received the Holy Spirit into my life. The next morning, I didn't wake up a saint. I woke up fearful of what I was capable of doing to my children. I felt the peace of trusting in God, knowing I wanted more than anything to be with Him in heaven. But I recognized my limitations as a human being.

Rage was not a limitation but a warning sign that I needed help. The peace of the Holy Spirit carried me through the next few days when my children were fussy, cried, or acted out. I tried to talk to Neal about what happened, but he brushed me off and made it clear that Ryan had done the same thing with him when I had left him alone with the boys the previous week. I didn't admit to him that I had nearly wrecked our son emotionally for life, nor did I manage to confide in him about the moment I surrendered to God on our bedroom floor.

Neal could only handle listening in spurts at the time—or, at least, that is what it felt like. Instead, he latched on to the fact Ryan had pooped twice outside of the toilet and managed to make a horrendous mess.

"Did you spank him?" he asked.

"No." I hid behind the shame of what I *had* almost done.

Silence was a coping mechanism. When my friends would call to dish about the latest gossip or complain about their boring and mundane days, I tuned them out. It didn't interest me to judge people for how they lived their lives or made their mistakes. I certainly couldn't judge.

Those who understood were a few women who had gone through the Bible study.

"I could die right now," I said when I was on the phone with Deidra, one of the younger women in the group.

"Shannon, don't say that. That's awful."

"No, no. That's not what I mean. I truly would be okay to die right now. I no longer fear death. I used to be so afraid to die, but now I look forward to the day I get to be with God forever."

"Oh, I don't know. I get what you mean, but I would hate to miss my kids growing up."

Missing out on my boys becoming young men, getting married, and having families of their own seemed so far off. Deidra didn't know the peace I'd felt in the surrender. I wanted to feel it forever.

I experienced moments of peace when I breastfed Seth and felt his little heartbeat pump in tandem with mine as we lay chest to chest. This would be interrupted by a scream of disdain and a little body hurtling itself on top of us to break the union. Out of reflex and habit, my hand shot out to block the full brunt of the attack, and one morning my reflex sent Ryan flying to the ground.

Ryan cried. Seth wailed. I grieved.

It was clear the opportunities for this peace were gone. I could no longer breastfeed Seth. It was detrimental to his safety and my relationship with Ryan. For once, I thought about my children first.

When Mother Nature called, I felt the weight of a few more pounds of anxiety. I couldn't have another baby. I was desperate in prayer. Psychologically, I could barely handle the two I already had. It wouldn't be fair to bring another baby into this crazy world. I couldn't go back on birth control. I didn't want to go back on the birth control pill. My weight ballooned, and my mood fluctuated, and something about it didn't feel right. However, I was desperate to keep from having another child I could potentially harm.

My friends were Protestant, but Neal and I agreed to bring up our family in the Catholic faith. This wasn't a difficult decision, but it was a lonely one. We did not really understand the Catholic Church but felt an inner sense of being at home when we attended Mass versus attending a worship service at one of our friends' Protestant churches. The Catholic Church comforted me. Church became my solace, the only place where I could pray to receive peace amidst the anxieties I felt with sex and in the possibility of having another baby.

Because of the different beliefs in our denominations, when I voiced concerns to friends about fertility and my need to put it on hold without going back on birth control, they couldn't understand my hesitation to do something more permanent. I felt like a child about to go against my parents' rules without understanding why they insisted on enforcing the rule.

I needed guidance from Dr. Baker and made an appointment.

"You realize the permanency of this decision?" she asked.

Her words steamrolled over my heart. *Permanent. No more children.* I blinked.

"I understand some couples have an ideal size for their family that works for them," she continued, "so I'm not trying to sway you one way or the other. However, I find it important to stress that though a vasectomy can be reversed, the odds of the reversal being effective are pretty low. And a tubal ligation pretty much seals the deal. I, for one, have not performed a reversal on a tubal ligation."

I shifted on the examining table, the paper crunching and crinkling beneath me.

"I don't think I can handle another baby," I said. I was unable to match my voice with the conviction in my gut. If she only knew what I was capable of, she would convince me to do the most permanent solution.

Her head tilted, and her eyes softened with understanding. She and I both had two children. She gave birth to her second child only a few months before she delivered Seth.

"Are you sleeping when the baby sleeps?" she asked.

I nodded. "I have both kids on a schedule. Seth takes a nap in the morning and afternoon, and Ryan takes one at the same time in the afternoon, so I get some rest then."

"Good." She wrote something down on her chart. "Do you find you are getting along okay in your day? Like, not sleeping more than usual but getting enough sleep?"

Again I nodded. "I've been getting up earlier than they both do in the morning to write in my journal. It's what keeps me going."

She smiled, and I could see her shoulders drop as if relieved. "Well, if you're able to get up early in the morning, then you're doing better than most people who *don't* have kids."

She scribbled on a notepad, tore off the sheet, and handed it to me. "Here is the name of a doctor I recommend to perform vasectomies. He is very efficient, and your husband will be in and out within a few hours."

"Thank you." I held on to the paper.

"Just remember," she said as she walked to the door. "You and your husband need to discuss this and make sure your family is where you want it to be."

The door closed, and I stared at the poster on the wall of the stages of embryonic gestation. *I wanted four kids.*

My stomach dropped. I pictured Ryan in one of his worst tantrums and felt the anxiety in my chest swell up like a helium balloon about to burst. *I can barely be the mother of two. How could I be a mother to four without royally screwing them up?*

Neal wasn't a hard sell. He admitted he'd hoped for a girl at some point, but he also felt the financial strain. I didn't have to convince him to go through with the surgery. My friends were supportive. They all understood, and a few had gone through the same discernment.

Natural Family Planning (NFP) is typically the Catholic Church's only option for birth control. It is the most natural form of birth control, using no medication and instead the ovarian cycle of the woman. At this time, I knew nothing about NFP. It was never mentioned in my family, so it didn't present as an option to explore. Most of my friends were not in the Catholic faith, and therefore it was not mentioned in any conversation I had when discerning this life-altering decision.

As a teenager, I was not informed on much about sex, birth control, or the options that were available. As a pre-teen in seventh grade, my parents sat me down and showed me the NOVA special on PBS about sex. There was not a follow-up discussion or a talk on safe sex, birth control, purity, chastity, abstinence, or any of the terms that would have been helpful at the time. My older sister's sexual prowess, along with the havoc her actions reaped upon our family when I was growing up, was the only underlying road map I'd been given. *Don't do what she did.* Plain and simple.

I knew a good Catholic girl waited to have sex until marriage; that much was imparted to me somewhere along the way. The Protestant youth group I attended through my tween years reinforced this message, but teen pregnancy wasn't as prevalent and it didn't come up in conversation.

However, as I suffered through high school, I'd been misinformed about abortion and protection. I was emotionally scarred from the trauma of experiencing a rape as a virgin, and I felt I severed the spiritual tie between myself and God. I was damaged goods. Once I fell into that lie and lived in shame, the only emotion that steered me on the outskirts of the right direction was fear of my father and fear of getting pregnant.

Two weeks after the rape in high school, my period didn't come. I sat balled up in a chair, hitting and kneading my hands into my stomach, terrified there was a pregnancy and I'd have to make the decision to either face my father or abort the baby. Thankfully, my period came the next day.

In college, when I walked away from the second rape and reported it to the police, I was in the clenches of terror when I had to wait on the blood tests to see if I was pregnant *and* if I was positive with HIV. I was blessed with an early period, but the wait for the results was as violating and traumatic as the actual rape.

The choice to call our family complete became easier as I acknowledged these interior scars and fears that caused an irrational displacement of hostility and anger. The decision not to bring another child into our family came from a place of love for my children and any future children I could have had. I knew I needed to trust in God's plan, but I also believed God had given me the wisdom to recognize when enough was enough.

One day prior to the surgery, I received a letter in the mail from the wife of one of Neal's co-workers. They lived in a town about an hour north of us in the Houston area, and I saw her once a year at a company picnic. She wrote:

> *My husband told me about Neal's impending procedure, and I felt called to share with you what the Catholic Church says in regards to this permanent form of birth control. I know it is not my place, but I can't help but feel as if you might regret this decision someday. Please pray about this.*

She included the following excerpt from the Catholic Catechism:

> *Periodic continence, that is, methods of birth regulation based on self-observation and the use of infertile periods, is in conformity with the objective criteria of morality. These methods respect the bodies of the spouses, encourage tenderness between them, and favor education of an authentic freedom. In contrast, "every action which, whether in anticipation of the conjugal act, or in its accomplishment, or in the development of its natural consequences, proposes, whether as an end or as a means, to render procreation impossible" is intrinsically evil.*[7]

---

7   *Catechism of the Catholic Church* (n.p.: Image Books, 1995), paragraph 2370.

Evil? Was she saying I was evil? Was the Catholic Church saying I was evil? The words of the highlighted text jumbled before me as my heart rate shot up with fury. How dare she? Who did she think she was, sticking her nose in our business? She didn't know the fear in my gut taunting me with the fact I wasn't cut out to be a mother.

Control—that's all it is, I thought. *Control.*

I crumpled up the note and threw it on the table so that Neal could see it.

"She means well," he said. He looked it over again. "Maybe she did something to prevent them from having more children and she regrets it. Maybe she doesn't want you to make the same mistake."

My mind screamed with frustration. Did she not realize I went back and forth with this in my mind over and over again? The memory of Ryan's big blue eyes the size of half-dollars staring up at me with fear kept me certain of the choice. A big family is not what God has planned. I assured myself, and put her note and uncertainty behind me.

However, when Neal walked out of the doctor's office drenched in sweat and incoherent from the extra dose of sedative, my heart sank with regret. Halfway through the surgery, they realized they had not numbed him entirely. He had felt the procedure as it took place. I was ashamed to have put him through the torture.

Did I make the wrong decision? The peace I longed for in preventing future harm on any children I could have did not settle over me with relief. I drove home with my husband passed out in the seat next to me, and I realized I had taken control. My heart sank.

God, save me from myself, I prayed.

CHAPTER 9
CALLED, NOT QUALIFIED

"All have sinned and are deprived of the glory of God."

Romans 3:23

The moment God met me on my bedroom floor in surrender to His will, His voice emerged from the depths of my spirit as if it had hibernated in a long devastating winter. Once I gave him my yes, there was no turning back. If my future decisions and losses had been laid out before me, I might have turned back.

Water pelted my face as I stood under the showerhead with my eyes closed.

Teach CCE.

The command was so loud and so real, it startled me, and I opened my eyes and gasped in a mouth full of water. Choking, I stepped out of the flow of water and grabbed at the tile wall for balance. It was mid-morning, Ryan was in his room watching *Thomas the Tank,* and Seth was down for his morning nap. The bathroom was so small, no one could slip in without bumping into me through the shower curtain.

Regardless, I stood still and listened. Water rushed from the showerhead and slapped against the porcelain tub. There was no other sound than my raspy breathing.

I am crazy.

I stepped back into the rushing water.

Teach CCE.

This time I couldn't mistake where it came from. It wasn't me, but it was *inside* of me. I felt everything implied with the simple statement. When I had cried out to God to change my life, I wasn't sure which denomination would nurture my faith, only that I was a Christian and everything else would be worked out later.

My later and God's later were on separate timetables. Teach CCE? Yes, I was crazy to even allow the thought to cross my mind. Whether I'd heard the voice of God or just uncovered a hidden longing to understand Him dwell up from some inner depth of my soul—either way, it was still crazy.

I knew nothing in detail about the Catholic faith to teach a class to kids.

All you need to know is My love.

Frustrated that my rare moment of silence and serenity had been invaded by this confusion, I flipped the shower knob off, squeezed the excess water from my newly cropped blonde hair, and grabbed a towel. Like a song stuck on instant replay. I heard. *Teach CCE. Teach CCE.*

Once dressed, I checked on Ryan and found that he had fallen asleep with his head next to the toy train track. Routine told me Seth had about a half-hour before he began to stir for lunch. *Teach CCE. Teach CCE.* My mind didn't stop. In the office, I grabbed a notepad and wrote it out: *Teach CCE. He is all I need to know.*

Finally, my mind went quiet. I stared at the words. Memories of Catholic catechism classes rushed forward. There were five of us. I was six years old, sitting at a table in a room as small as a bedroom closet. The teacher, the mom of the girl sitting next to me, held a plastic box that looked like a big television screen. She put in a tape, and we watched bible stories come to life as the cartoon pictures scrolled across the screen, one scene at a time. It was primitive but mesmerizing.

I got older and we moved. I was in Catholic school, which meant catechism was an actual religion class with notebooks, tests, and Mass every Wednesday. I volunteered to read the Bible at Mass only because I loved to read aloud. We learned to sing the Our Father and sign it as well. The guitar choir played the Alleluia, which was fun and a change of pace from the stuffy organ.

Catholic school ended when I was in middle school, and once again I was in a classroom with someone's parent reading from a book and still more tests. *Whah, whah, whah.* They droned like the famous unseen Peanuts cartoon teacher.

The older I got, the more I cared about who was in the class rather than what I was learning from the class. By the time I was in high school, I felt severed from God.

How did any of this qualify me to teach children what I had walked away from?

A faint babble came from Seth's room. I put the notebook back on the desk and dismissed the wistfulness that settled in my chest and pushed the thought away.

Sunday morning, the boys were up, fed, and dressed. There was no excuse to avoid attending Mass. The last time I'd been to Mass, I'd left Ryan in the nursery only to be told he bit the other kids and had bad behavior.

Mortified and embarrassed, I grabbed Ryan from the nursery worker's arms. "Have you been bad?" I asked him.

Her mouth dropped open. "Don't say that. *Ryan* is not bad. His *behavior* is bad."

My cheeks flamed. I grabbed my son and vowed to never go back.

This morning, my chest puffed forward with pride as I held on to Ryan's hand and neared the nursery. The smile on the nursery attendant's face didn't waver when Ryan and I walked into the little room.

"Ryan." She knelt to his eye level. "I haven't seen you in a while. I'm so glad you're here."

I could tell she meant it. My chest deflated, and I relaxed. She cared about him, and that's all that mattered.

"I love you, buddy," I said. I gave him a kiss before he wriggled free to play.

Seth was asleep on Neal's shoulder when I found them in the main sanctuary. It was as if the two edges of a zipper came together, the grooves meshing perfectly within the pattern, sealing what was once undone. The choir belted out songs of prayer that were familiar from my childhood, calling my spirit out from the depths of hibernation. The Scripture readings linked with the music as the Word of God fed my malnourished spirit. Receiving the Eucharist brought me back to my knees and the fresh memory of surrender.

Neal looked over at me every now and then as I wiped a tear away from the corner of my eye. Seth stirred only a few times, but Neal held on to him, which gave me a moment to embrace the peace. When did the Mass change? I shook my head in reply to my own ignorance. The Mass hadn't changed. I had.

The priest stood to pronounce the final blessing, but the deacon had an announcement to make. "Classes for CCE will begin the second weekend of September. The CCE office is in need of volunteers to teach all grade levels. If you are interested in learning more about volunteering, there will be an information meeting tonight at 7 p.m. in the Family Life Center."

My heart beat like I'd finished a marathon. Every hair on my body stood on end. *Teach CCE*, I heard again, just as I had earlier in the week. I looked over at Neal with Seth nuzzled in the crook of his neck. What would hurt if I went to the meeting?

I leaned into him. "I think I want to go to that meeting."

His eyebrows shot up before he nodded in answer.

The priest gave the final blessing.

"When are the classes?" Neal asked on our way to get Ryan from the nursery.

I shrugged. "I guess I'll find out tonight. I'm not committing yet, but I am interested in seeing if maybe it's something I would want to do."

Full of nervous energy, I bathed Ryan and got him ready for bed so Neal didn't have to wrestle with him for the evening. Seth was fed and already sleepy-eyed when I kissed him on the forehead before leaving.

God, I sure hope you know what you're doing, I prayed.

I pulled into the church parking lot. This was my doing, and I knew it. Not long after the evening I had cried out to God to do something with my life, I had confessed another truth. *God, I'm not sure which church I want to belong to,* I prayed. *Do I stay with all of my new friends or remain Catholic?*

Some of the women from the Bible study had invited me to do Breaking Free again because the general consensus was that most of us would get more from it if we were to go through the study one more time, knowing what we were getting ourselves into.

Even still, I knew I couldn't walk out on my Catholic faith again. Talking aloud, as if God stood right beside me, I made a plea: "If you want me to remain Catholic, then help me to be interested in the faith. Help me to understand it."

Now here I was "called" to attend an information meeting about *teaching* the Catholic faith, not necessarily *learning* it. God had a sense of humor.

I walked through the doors of the Family Life Center, expecting to sit down and listen to what was expected of a Catholic catechism teacher. Instead, I was signed in and asked, "What grade do you want to teach?"

"Uh, um . . . "

Where did I need to begin? Which grade did they learn "Jesus Loves Me"? That would have been the appropriate starting point and what I could probably handle.

A woman walked up to the table as I fumbled with an answer. "I think you would be perfect for high school." She smiled. "How would you like to assist John with eleventh and twelfth grade CCE?"

They didn't know my name, and I was already typecast. I got it. I was young—the youngest in the room, for sure—and I was present. Two criteria met, and I was in. Before I could answer, the woman took me by the arm and led me to the side.

"I'm Theresa, the youth minister," she said. She was older than me and had an air about her that was both peaceful and confident.

"I'm Shannon Deitz."

She leaned in conspiratorially. "I've seen you in Mass, and I've always wanted to meet you. There is something about you that told me I might see you in here one day."

I stepped back, physically shocked. "Really?"

Inside, I thought, *You have no idea who I am and where I've been.*

She smiled and nodded. "I think you're what our teenagers need. Someone young and new. Come on. I'll introduce you to John."

John was the father of three, two teenagers and one not far behind. He seemed grateful to have the help, and instead of listening to the meeting he pulled me aside into the classroom. He gave me a book and explained the lessons. He'd begin with the first one, since they knew him and he had been teaching before. I was assigned the second lesson. We'd meet on Sunday evenings, with the first one starting in two weeks.

In less than an hour, I left the Family Life Center with a workbook in my hands and an assignment. What had just happened?

"Jesus Christ as Living Water" was the theme of the chapter I was assigned. I read the first chapter John was scheduled to teach and pored over the second, going deeper into the symbolism of water within our faith—baptism and blessings.

There was so much to learn, and I was pleased to recall some of the teaching from my childhood. It felt like I'd received the key that opened a locked treasure chest that I'd had in my possession for years but had stored and put away, only to be forgotten. The more I read, the more clear the message became. It was simple and yet profound.

After reading the chapter, I visualized the water of mercy that had cleansed me only a few months before as I cried out for God to take my life. I'd been drenched as a child with the holy waters of baptism, I had received Christ in First Communion, and as a young adult I had declared my belief in the faith and received the Holy Spirit within

Confirmation. But it wasn't until I surrendered to God that I fully embraced the gifts that protected my soul.

One week before our first class, I received a phone call from my mom late at night.

"Shannon, I'm sorry to tell you." I heard her pull the phone away and sob. "Jason killed himself. I just got the call and I thought you'd want to know."

Jason was a friend from high school, one of my few Catholic friends. He was a year younger, but we had been in the same CCE class. Ironically, I was his Confirmation sponsor, the person he chose to put a hand on his shoulder as he accepted and said yes to God and to our Catholic faith. We were children. He chose me because we were comrades in the unknown. He looked up to me because I played the part well, as if I knew more about our faith. I took our friendship seriously, but I was blind to the responsibility of guiding him through the sacrament and how to grow in faith.

Now he was gone.

The grief threatened to tear me into shreds. Somewhere along my years of growing up in the faith, I was under the impression we went to hell if we committed suicide. But I couldn't fathom his soul lost in the depths of hell because he had taken his own life.

Jason can't be in hell! I screamed into a pillow, the sobs wracking my body.

Neal didn't know what to do or say, except to suggest that I call Fr. Richard. The next morning, I called him once Seth was down for his morning nap. I needed to know before I called Jason's mother.

He was unable to take my call, but I was told Fr. Richard would call at his earliest convenience. Intermittently, the tears flowed between diaper changes, feedings, and building train tracks.

"Why you sad, Mommy?" Ryan put a chubby hand up to my wet cheek. Sensing my obvious melancholy, he was more in tune to me and how I felt than insisting on unobtainable tasks or requests that inevitably ended up with a head-banging tantrum. It was a reprieve.

Late that afternoon, Fr. Richard returned the call, and when I told him what had happened, there was a deep sigh.

"I am sorry for your loss," he said. "It is tragic to lose someone as young as he, but to lose him to suicide is all the more devastating."

A whimper escaped my lips. "Is he in hell?" I sounded like a five-year-old girl hearing about death for the first time.

He sighed again. "The Catholic Church has come a long way in response to suicide. The Church realizes it cannot ignore the many cases of mental health that result in an unclear and unstable mind. Because of this, it truly depends on the mind-set of the individual. Were they depressed? Were they of sound mind when they made the decision to take their lives? If this is the case and they suffered from mental illness, then the death is a tragic loss but one the Church recognizes and treats as a loss that is worth the same dignity and burial on consecrated ground as any other death."

"So he's *not* in hell?" Hope filled my heart.

"No, I'm pretty certain he is not. There is a hell, but it is not for us to contemplate who among us will spend our time in the internal inferno." He cleared his throat. "This young man's family moved away not long after I became the pastor here, but from what little I know they are a good family. I'll say a prayer for the repose of Jason's soul in Mass tomorrow morning."

For the first time all day, I felt at peace. "Thank you," I said.

The call to Jason's mom wasn't as daunting now that I knew he wasn't condemned.

"Shannon, Jason was a tortured soul," she told me. "One minute he was high and life was good. In the next breath, he'd tear about the house like a maniac on a rampage. We tried to get him help. He was seeing a counselor. I don't know why he'd do this."

The sound of a mother's grief cuts deep.

"Jason was a good guy," I said. I knew she didn't hear anything else. No words could bring her the comfort she longed to hold onto.

What if we had remained close? Could I have helped him? I wept over the years I'd lost contact with Jason and how he'd chosen me to stand with him in his faith and I didn't follow through.

The time for the first CCE class arrived. I was thirty minutes early and sat alone in the empty classroom for twenty minutes. Ten minutes before class, John came in with his teenage son, a junior in high school. I blinked. He looked like Jason. I swallowed heard and mentally shut the door to my sadness.

A few minutes later, a few more boys sauntered into the room. They high-fived John and crowded around him as they talked about football. Clumps of girls filed into the room. They whispered amongst themselves and gave me the once-over before circling up at the back of the room.

I was transported back to high school, to the awkward moment of being the only one left alone, the odd ball, the only one not in on the joke. Heat rose up my neck.

Finally, John called the class together and made the girls move out of their circle to join the rest of the class.

"This year I have an assistant." He gestured toward me. "Her name is Shannon Deitz, so you guys be nice to her, okay?"

They regarded me with little interest. A few girls not a part of the "inner circle" group sat alone along the edge of the room and offered a welcoming smile. I smiled back and did my best to fake confidence.

John made a few announcements and allowed the kids to go around the room, introducing themselves, before he started the lesson. I observed the dynamics of the group to pick up on the body language of the various groupings of kids. It had been a decade since I was in their shoes, but it felt as if I were sucked through some unseen vortex and that a younger version of myself sat in front of them, on display.

My nerves flared when it was my turn to share a little about myself. I was tempted to shrug my shoulders with feigned indifference and give some smart-aleck comment about being a young mom. It was my go-to defense move: when nervous, shy, or insecure, say something witty and deflect the attention.

"Hi, I'm Shannon," I said.

Twenty pairs of eyes looked at me. They were interested, or so it seemed.

"I am married and have two little boys—Ryan, who is about to turn three, and Seth, who is six months old."

The girls gave a collective "Aww" when I mentioned the kids.

This eased the moment, and before I knew it I said something I hadn't planned. "It hasn't been long since I've been in your shoes, so I hope that maybe this year we can learn something together."

There were a few nods from the boys and smiles from the girls. John clapped his hands together and took it from there.

"Okay, let's get started then."

He opened the workbook to chapter one—and read.

In each chapter was a lesson, questions for the group, a suggested activity, and a prayer. But we listened to John read the entire lesson. Eyes closed, girls doodled, and the boys stared up and counted ceiling tiles. The question session revived them, but the content of the lesson had been lost to most. I was stuck in the vortex and back in the same CCE class I sat through in high school.

This has to change, I thought. It wasn't that John's heart wasn't in it. It was clear the kids adored and respected him and that he'd taught it this way for years. The teens' blank stares triggered me and I felt a desire to show them something *more*.

I reviewed the lesson I was to teach again and couldn't help but think about the moments Jason sat next to me in class. We'd pass notes while the parent, teacher, or nun read the lesson. We solved the world's problems via secret script, more concerned about the ins and outs of our love lives than the salvation of our souls.

Did he turn to You, God? Did Jason pray and ask You for help? Were You speaking to him but he couldn't hear You?

Before me, as if played out on a movie screen, I imagined Jason in the last minutes of his life. *Wow.*

I came out of the trance. Without hesitation, I grabbed my pen and wrote it all down. It was clear to me. I needed the teens to understand what I'd witnessed.

Sunday evening came, and every nerve in my body was ablaze with anticipation. In Mass I prayed for the confidence needed to deliver the message in the way I felt God called me to carry it out. It was only a room of twenty teenagers, but I was petrified.

They sauntered into the room, some already in their groups, while others ate the last bites of the meal the church served in the Family Life Center. John hadn't arrived, and panic set in. Was he making me lead the entire class alone?

Then I saw his son enter the room, with John following behind.

He smiled. "You ready?"

I nodded, afraid to speak for fear I'd lose the little thread of courage I had to do the lesson.

"All right, then, let's get them gathered for opening prayer."

He whistled and motioned everyone to come closer to us in the front of the room, where all of the couches and chairs were. "Tonight Shannon is going to do the lesson," he said, "so let's bow our heads and pray an Our Father and a blessing over Shannon."

The room got quiet and everyone prayed the Our Father in unison. John put his hand on my shoulder, and I felt a few more hands touch my back. I closed my eyes and concentrated on John's prayer.

"Heavenly Father, fill Shannon with Your peace. Guide her and direct her. Come, Holy Spirit. Be with us this evening. Open our hearts to Your message. In Jesus's name we pray, amen."

My body relaxed. I prayed silently, *Father, please let at least one person here get something from what you've given me.*

I opened my eyes and felt an eagerness to get started.

I needed room to move around. I made everybody get out of their comfortable chairs and couches to sit in a half-circle on the floor. I opened the workbook to chapter 2 and read a bit of the lesson that went into our thirst for truth and how Christ, as Living Water, can fulfill this thirst. I looked at the group and witnessed what I had witnessed the week before: yawns, tops of heads as they scribbled on notes, blank stares.

Then I closed the book.

"When I was seventeen, I sat in a room like this and listened to the same lesson. When I looked over it again for this week, I was surprised to remember a few details about baptism, but most of it felt new."

A few teens were still preoccupied, but I had the attention of the majority of the room.

"I didn't listen to the lessons, because it didn't feel like they mattered. I was already baptized. I went to Mass every Sunday. Why did I need to listen?

"I even became the sponsor for Confirmation of a good guy friend of mine, Jason. It was like the blind leading the blind."

I laughed and heard a few courteous giggles.

"He chose me because he knew I wouldn't make a big deal about all the rules we needed to follow. Jason and I became close friends that year. We spent the majority of our CCE class writing back and forth on notes like that." I pointed to a note that a young man passed to the girl behind him.

In embarrassment, he put his head between his knees. The class laughed.

"We helped each other get through some issues. His girlfriend was crazy." I made a funny face and with the response I could see I had the guys' attention. "And he encouraged me when I was down, which was a lot my senior year."

My throat tightened, and I knew it would be hard to get through the lesson without tears.

"Jason passed away last week."

The room went quiet.

"He committed suicide."

I let a few tears fall. John jumped up from his chair and grabbed a tissue. He handed it to me. "Are you okay? You don't have to do this."

I took the tissue. "I'm good. I need to do this."

I looked at the kids. Every pair of eyes in the room was on me.

"When I first went over this lesson, I realized the gift we have in our sacraments. The security of being baptized, the weekly gift we receive in Communion, and then to have the help of the Holy Spirit in Confirmation. I didn't get it when I was your age. I don't think Jason did either."

I cleared my throat and felt a wave of fresh energy wash over me. "But when I got the call that Jason committed suicide, I was devastated. I was afraid he'd go to hell." I saw a few nods in the room. "A priest helped me realize that's not our place to assume. I don't know Jason's state of mind when he died, but I do know he was depressed. When I looked over this lesson again, I couldn't help but picture what might have happened."

I put the book down and brought a chair to the center of the room. I began to share what I had seen.

"Jason is in his room, sitting at his desk, hunched over the paper that held his final message, his body physically tired from the pain of depression, his heart splintered in his chest in a million pieces, too daunting to find a way to mend."

I saw Jason in the chair as I explained my vision to the teens. With words, I showed the scene.

"Jesus appears behind him. His hands rest on Jason's shoulders. Light illuminates from Jesus, pulsating and growing brighter. The light is an energy that takes on a life of its own and pours over Jason like a waterfall. An invisible barrier surrounds Jason and blocks the light from seeping through, keeping Jason from healing."

My voice cracked.

Not a sound could be heard in the room—not a rustle of paper, a yawn, or a sigh. They sat straight and leaned in. John brought me a cup of water.

"The barrier keeps Jason from hope and truth. Mistakenly defeated, he gets up from his desk and follows through with his plan."

I stood by the chair and imagined I was Jesus, with Jason in my arms. I couldn't stop.

"In the end, Jesus weeps. Holding on to Jason's tortured soul, Jesus cradles him as a mother would her newborn child, and the light of His tears covers Jason's soul, embracing him in eternal life and making all things new."

I looked into their wet eyes and felt the pain, the loneliness, and the understanding of what Jason might have been feeling, and my spirit came alive with a great desire to make the message clear.

I stood up to speak, reinforcing what the lesson in the book said but giving it to them in a way I needed to hear it when I was their age.

"Christ *is* our living water. *There is always hope.* The enemy tries to distort that message and make us think we aren't good enough, we aren't worthy, we can never overcome the depression. But those are lies. Jesus is *always* with us, and His mercy breaks those barriers when we invite Him in. We *can't* give up."

A fire I'd never felt before burst forth from within.

"*Even if,*" I said. "Even if you've been diagnosed with bipolar disorder. Even if you've gotten so far behind in school you can't keep your grades up. Even if you feel alone because your best friend ditched you for another group. Even if your girlfriend or boyfriend cheated and doesn't want to date you anymore. Good riddance!"

There was a spattering of laughter.

"Even if you've been carrying the shame of a dark secret since childhood."

All of these scenarios and emotions slammed into my spirit like a freight train. The last time I'd felt the emotions of those around me this intense was when I was nine years old with my face down on the altar carpet of my aunt's church. I was filled with a desperation for them to know the freedom of following Christ.

"Christ is always here," I said. "Christ is *always* pouring out His light upon you, but we have to *want* to make the move to receive it, to let His light cover us and soak in."

I took the cup of water and held it up for them.

"I'm thirsty. John gave me this cup of water to drink to quench my thirst, but in order for it to work I have to take a drink." I drank the cup of water. "John and I are here to do our best to teach you more about Christ. We are handing you a cup of water, but it's up to you to take it and consume it."

Kids toppled on top of each other to get their questions out. Many wanted to know more about the Church's teaching on suicide and when did I think Jason walked away from feeling like there was any hope. It was a great discussion, and it was obvious it hit home for many.

Afterward, once everyone had gone, a young woman came up to me. "I've been there before," she said. She bent her head in shame. "I couldn't go through with it."

I reached out and brought her into an embrace. "I'm so glad you didn't. You are such a beautiful woman, and I know God has great plans for you."

Her body shook with sobs. I held her until she calmed down. She looked up at me. "Thank you."

In bed that night, I thought about the young woman who felt such sadness she wanted to take her life. I understood. And I understood why God had called me to teach CCE—if not for growth in my knowledge of the Catholic Church, then to help other teens get through what might be the hardest part of life.

CHAPTER 10

THE SCREAM

"Stop judging by appearances, but judge justly."

John 7:24

Each week that I had a lesson to teach, I would pore over the readings, the suggested activities, and the prayers and then sit back and think, *If I were sixteen again and they were teaching me this, what was going on in my life that would have helped me to hear the lesson?*

John changed things up, too, bringing a bit more creativity into his teaching. After a few Sundays, our class got bigger. Kids were bringing their friends.

Teaching the CCE class was something I looked forward to, and it didn't take long before Theresa approached me to help with the high school youth activities and retreats. In many ways, I was a teenager again, getting a chance to rewrite history, and this time I was the one with the courage to lead the others in the right path. I saw the spirit of each and every kid, regardless of their background, their social status, or their perceived intelligence. Their spirit is what gripped me, and I wanted them to recognize their worth.

My spirit burned with a passion I had never felt before. If I could do anything to help these kids, I was going to do it. At home, I spoke incessantly about the kids, their issues, and the lessons I learned along with them.

Neal supported my work with the teens, but he didn't get what fueled my passion. When I tried to get us involved at church with adult Bible groups or small circles, he would come along, but it was a fight every step of the way. I was desperate for us to be on the same page spiritually, for him to come along with me on this journey, but he felt what I was doing was more of a hobby and one that didn't need to include him.

A slow but deliberate hairline crack formed between us. This added to the layered issues of sexual intimacy and petty disagreements that were already there between us.

Instead of a kiss hello when Neal walked in the door, an argument would ensue.

"Why is it so important to go to the Joneses for dinner tonight?" he might say. "We don't know them."

"Yes, we do," I'd reply. "They sit next to us every Sunday. Quit acting like it's the end of the world. It's a spiritual dinner club."

"Yeah, with people we don't know. This is not what I wanted to do on a Friday night."

"But what about what *I* want to do? We *always* hang out with *your* friends. Why can't we make friends together?" Animosity and frustration boiled in my blood. My voice rose octaves higher than was needed for a simple argument.

It could be a different circumstance but the fight would remain the same. Neal would storm back into the room where I was, or at times we'd be nose to nose, neither backing down.

"We *always* hang out with my friends?" he'd say. "*Always*? What about the Bible study you drag me to? Or the stupid potluck dinners? And God forbid we try to get out of Mass at a decent time. You have to stay and talk to everyone on your way out."

I couldn't fathom why he'd be adverse to events that were meant to bring us together. It felt like the more I tried to encourage a spiritual connection between us, the further we drifted apart.

God had ahold of my heart, and though I knew I needed to bring Neal into the fold with us, I still held on to pride. It was easier to add a layer to the wall between us and focus my efforts on Ryan.

Ryan's destructive and aggressive behaviors grew more intense with each month. A special on autism aired on the morning news, and I couldn't help but correlate it to Ryan on all fours, rocking and humming when he was upset, or when he banged his head on the back of the couch.

"Neal, I want to check out that autism school that's near us," I told him one day. "Before we put Ryan in the pre-K3 classes."

He threw his hands in the air. "There is nothing wrong with Ryan. He is a boy. That's all. When are you going to let this go?"

I'm not wrong.

Neal's lack of support for my mother's instinct left me lonely and frustrated. And it was my instinct alone. A few months earlier, I had managed to convince the pediatrician to get us into a specialized clinic at Texas Children's Hospital to do an evaluation on Ryan. The pediatricians at Texas Children's Hospital witnessed Ryan in the midst of a meltdown, a tantrum so intense it sent him underneath the table, rocking on all fours and humming, because he didn't want to put the blocks in the order the doctors asked.

Normally my blood temperature would rise and I'd be embarrassed by the behavior, but I rejoiced in the action. *Thank you, God! They see him at his worse, and they will help us.*

A week later, we received a letter that explained he was a normal, hyperactive little boy who had a mother possibly suffering from postpartum depression.

I *wasn't* depressed. My heart sunk. Why wouldn't anyone believe me and help Ryan?

I didn't *want* to find something wrong with Ryan. I wanted to figure out if there was something we could *do* for him. He was three and almost ostracized socially. I didn't want him to continue through life one step behind because no one fought for him. Being shunned and classified as "different" was not a future I wanted for my son.

"Let me take him to the school for at least a few weeks," I pleaded. "Let's give it a chance. If it is clear to me he isn't autistic, then I'll take him out."

Neal left the room, resigned. "Do what you want."

The first visit was more of a consultation, a trial meeting to see if Ryan fit the criteria to be in the school. At three years old, he had an exemplary vocabulary but couldn't look anyone in the eye. He rocked on all fours, hummed, and beat his head against the wall. The fact that he could communicate with words set him apart from the usual autistic spectrum, but the rest of his behaviors were near textbook.

Mrs. Ford smiled as Ryan ran outside in the playground area. "It is clear to me Ryan isn't autistic," she said.

Ryan hid in the belly of a cement tube that served as a tunnel for an obstacle course.

"His speech is exceptional, and I can see many ways in which he is trying to communicate but doesn't have the right words."

My heart rose and fell in one swift moment, grateful Ryan wasn't going to spend his life struggling with the label of autism, yet defeated because that meant everyone else was right. It was me. I was Ryan's problem.

"Now," she continued, "I wouldn't be surprised if he had Asperger's syndrome, which is on the same spectrum as autism, but they are high functioning and often brilliant kids. Their issues are more on social and sensory integration."

Suspended in uncertainty, I looked over at the mouth of the cement tube, searching for signs of Ryan emerging into the real world.

"So what do I do?" I asked.

"I'd love to have him come a few days a week with some of our older students. His vocabulary and communication skills are so good, I think he could help the other kids, plus we can work on the sensory issues."

Desperate, I took her up on the offer and enrolled Ryan for two days a week. We didn't have the money, but that didn't matter. I owed him everything.

One afternoon I went to pick Ryan up from his new school. A little five-year-old boy waited to be picked up as well. He wouldn't look at me or talk to me when the teacher tried to introduce us. Instead, he held his hands up to his face, fingers spread apart, and clapped. Ryan saw this as a behavior to imitate.

I gently took his hand and walked him out to the car. When we got to the car, he froze like a statue and refused to bend a limb to get into the backseat. He already weighed at least fifty pounds, which felt even heavier when I picked him up because of the resistance. Once in the backseat, in a glass-shattering, high-pitched tone, he screamed.

Seth, who was asleep in his carrier, woke and wailed in unison. Sweat trickled down my face and from my armpits as I did everything I could to get him to bend his body and sit in the car seat. For five minutes, Ryan's arms were plastered to his side and his scream sucked the oxygen from the air.

Defeated, I crawled out of the back seat, slammed the car door, and fell against it, unable to stand up because the sobs stole my strength.

"Is there anything I can do to help?" I heard the teacher ask from the doorway of the school. I looked up and saw her standing there with the little boy at her side.

I shook my head. "No," I managed. "He'll stop in a minute."

But I wasn't certain he would. I took a deep breath and opened the back door.

Leaning all the way inside without physically climbing in, I yelled above his scream. "Ryan, if you'll let me buckle you in, I'll get you a new train!".

A whoosh of air filled the car with silence. Ryan cooperated and relaxed. Even Seth's cry turned to a feeble whimper.

With trembling fingers, I buckled him in and managed to get behind the wheel without losing the last thread of patience that kept me from insanity. It was a short ten-minute ride home, but both boys were asleep when I pulled into the driveway. In a state of rest, it was easy to see how delicate and fragile their lives were in my hands.

I pulled Seth's carrier out of the car first and placed him in his room, still asleep in the carrier, and went back for Ryan. I leaned in and put my hands underneath Ryan's armpits and hoisted him into my arms without waking him up. I sat on the edge of his bed and stared at the face that resembled my own.

What am I going to do?

That weekend I left the boys alone with Neal for two days while I chaperoned my first youth retreat. Theresa asked if I would give a talk for the retreat, and she needed another adult chaperone. More than willing to get a weekend away from my responsibilities as a mom, I agreed and prepared for the talk on the gift of the Holy Spirit known as right judgment.

For the first time, I felt called to speak about the first rape.

"I admit I wasn't an angel when it came to my relationship with Paul," I began. "I flirted. I promised things I knew I wouldn't carry out. I felt it was what he wanted to hear, and I was desperate to be loved. I had turned away from the love of God and looked to man to fulfill the void.

"But." I paused and walked away from the podium. "That doesn't give Paul the right to have taken something precious from me when I said no.

"I did not want what happened that day in his room. Yes, I had placed myself there. Yes, I had made empty promises. But I said no. And what he took from me that day was not his to take.

"When I walked away that day, I felt I severed the final tie between God and me. That was the enemy speaking to my heart, because there is nothing I—or *you*—can do to ever make God love me—or *you*—less.

"My judgment was off. I did not respect myself or know the Holy Spirit that was within me. I listened to the enemy's lies and believed I was not worthy of God's love and redemption. There are many actions of mine I would

142

change if I could go back, but most importantly I wish I would've talked about what happened. But the shame kept me silent."

All eyes were on me. Adrenaline pumped through my veins, and I felt the Spirit within me rise.

"Had I spoken and admitted to someone what happened despite the decisions I made to put myself in that situation, I know I would've received the help I needed. Instead, I chose to listen to the lies of the enemy and continued to walk down the dark path of self-destruction."

Girls wiped tears away. Boys bent their heads, unable to look at me.

"The gift I have now is that today is a new day. I am renewed in Christ. I am learning to use the gift of right judgment to follow God's will *daily*. Trust the gifts of the Spirit that is within you to hear God's voice and make the right choices."

I delivered the talk on the first morning, and throughout the day the kids came up to me and thanked me for what I'd said. With every hint of praise, I got flustered and brushed it off. "It's not me, it's God," I said.

I didn't want to receive praise, because I didn't feel worthy of receiving such praise for offering the truth of my bad decisions. I believed everything I said to the teens but knew I was still a work in progress accepting it for myself.

Victoria, a teen we'd hired to babysit the boys from time to time, came up and gave me a hug.

"Can I talk to you alone?" she asked.

There were rules in place at the church that said no adult could be alone with a child unless they were in a room with other adults and could be seen. Considering what I'd been through in my past, I was happy the church had such rules in place. We walked over to a corner of the meeting hall and sat down on the carpet.

"You said something in your talk that really got to me today," she said.

She was a striking young woman, with dark brown hair that fell like satin to her waist and wide eyes that matched the same deep, rich brown of her hair. She was one of the girls that came into CCE with an entourage of girls around her. She was never alone. Often she'd come wearing her volleyball uniform, having come from a game or practice, but she rarely missed a class.

She was the same type of girl I wanted to be when I was her age. Cool and confident. The fact I reached her through the talk made me sit up a bit. "Really?" I asked.

Victoria looked down and nodded. "You said you believe you could have saved yourself from a lot of bad stuff if you had only talked about what happened to you?"

She needed me to expand.

"I know I can't go back," I said.

She looked away again and kept busy picking at the threads of carpet.

"But I think about how I behaved after I was raped. I felt like I wasn't worth anything, so I acted that way too."

Big sorrowful eyes looked up at me.

I continued. "I can't help but think if I had said something to someone and maybe gotten help that I wouldn't
have made some of the bad decisions that caused even more
hurt in my life."

Victoria nodded again and picked at the carpet.

It was clear she had something she wanted to share. I
empathized with how hard talking about whatever it was
that troubled her could be.

God, please give me the right words to say, I prayed.

"You know you can talk to me, right?" I said.

She nodded. We sat like that, me with my back against
the wall, staring at her bent head as she picked the threads
of worn carpet, for what felt like many minutes.

"What if you aren't sure about something?" she said.
"Like, what if you don't know if something is bad or not?"

Deep inside, it was clear to me this young girl hurt in
ways that affected her deeply. I felt like we were balancing
our way along a tightrope and with one swift move we'd
both come tumbling down.

"Well, I guess the first question to ask yourself is how
does whatever 'it' is make you feel?" I said. "If it makes you
feel shame or uncomfortable or even angry or hurt, then
whether it's considered right or wrong, it is still important
to talk about it."

Again she nodded.

We balanced through another stretch of silence when
she finally looked up again. "Thanks, Shannon. I guess I
need to think about some things."

She got up off the floor and went to join a circle of giggling girls.

My heart pounded. What was she not telling me?

The following week, I made a point to talk to Ryan's teacher about the habits he picked up from the other children with more severe cases of autism.

"He is doing so well," the teacher said. "His presence here has been great for the other kids because he vocalizes perfectly. I know they have their habits, and I'm sure Ryan is picking up on those, but give him some time. I really think we are making progress."

Anxiety festered in me all day, and I couldn't get my mind off Ryan and what was best for him or Victoria and what it was she wanted to divulge. Both children suffered silently, and in both cases I felt powerless to help.

When I picked up Ryan that afternoon, he let out a scream that would make any horror film producer proud, and again I fought, forced, and pleaded for him to get into his car seat for the ride home. And the new behaviors made their way home.

Ryan sat at the dinner table and screamed. With his fingers wide, he clapped his hands. He didn't want to eat his peas.

"That's it." Neal threw his napkin on the table. "I've had it with this school. He didn't do that before he went in. We're taking him out."

He said this with such a finality that I knew not to argue. I wasn't sure I *wanted* to argue at this point. Neal was right. Ryan wasn't autistic. It was time to face the truth: the problem was me.

In desperate need of a night out, Neal and I got a babysitter, which lent a great excuse to have Victoria come over. She'd begged to babysit the boys, and I figured maybe it was also because she wanted more of a chance to talk.

She came by an hour before her time to babysit. I was dressed and ready to go for the evening and was getting the boys fed and ready for bed when Neal let her in. He excused himself to take a shower, which left us time to talk.

"I brought some pictures of my birthday party we had last weekend," she said. "Do you want to see?"

"Sure."

I stopped what I was doing and took the pictures. The first was of Victoria with a man who didn't look old enough to be her father but wasn't young enough to be a brother either. They sat next to one another on a bench.

"Who is that?" I asked.

"That's my volleyball trainer."

She reached down to take the picture away. She pointed out her brothers and her mom and dad, and in every picture she was in, the trainer was next to her or close by.

A weird feeling invaded the pit of my stomach. I didn't want to jump to conclusions, but it seemed odd that her sports trainer would be so close in all of the pictures.

"How long has that guy been your trainer?" I asked.

She fiddled with the pictures and put them in her backpack. "Um, I guess it's been since I was nine, I think." A flicker of sadness made her eyes dull and face fall. "Yeah, it's been about five years. We do everything together. My mom even lets me go to tournaments with him."

My pulse quickened. "You mean tournaments where you have to stay overnight somewhere?"

She looked away and nodded.

The air in the room was stale. It was as if I could feel God stopping time so that we could have this conversation. "Would you stay in the same room with him?"

She kept her eyes down. "Yeah, but, you know, I slept in a separate bed. He does everything with us. My parents love him."

"Is he married?"

She looked up then, and I could see we had reached the end of the conversation. "He was, but they've been divorced for awhile. So, where are you going tonight?"

Months passed, and each day felt like a continual recurrence of the day before. We took Ryan out of the autism school and enrolled him in pre-K3 classes at the Catholic school. Intellectually, he surpassed the other kids, but socially he received "reds" and warnings every day. I exhausted efforts trying to come up with incentives for him—behavior charts with "Way to Go!" and "You Rock!" stickers for the days he came home with a "green," which meant no warning, and stars for the days he managed a "yellow." If he received so many for the week, then we got to go to the McDonald's playground that weekend.

Little did Ryan know that taking the kids to the indoor playground was more of a reward for *me*. Seth was a one-year-old with places to go. He had the same energy and curiosity as Ryan without the unexplained tantrums. He had a smile on his face from the moment he woke up to the moment he fell asleep. If he got upset, he let you know, but he was easily pacified.

Summer edged closer, which meant the CCE classes and youth retreats and activities were coming to an end. The teens did mission trips and conferences during the summer, but I knew those would require more time than Neal was willing to give.

Victoria babysat more often, which gave Neal and me time to get out of the house and mingle with friends, and that helped us reconnect, but the evenings often led to bickering and arguing. The highs and lows of our marriage were exhausting; there were many days my future looked bleak enough that during idle time, thoughts crept in of what my life would be like as someone else. I envied everyone around me who appeared to be better off financially, with husbands who had high-profile jobs and who lived in the newer homes in decent neighborhoods.

I had girlfriends, but I couldn't explain what I felt to them because I didn't want them to think of me as a jealous, envious, or ungrateful person. I didn't want them to know we struggled to keep up. I was ashamed, which led me to feel even *more* ashamed.

The only sense of worth I felt inside came in the moments I worked with the teens. I embraced the truth of God and felt empowered when I shared it with the girls who talked with me about their issues. One of the teens couldn't stop cutting to release anger, and I was able to find a way to bring the issue of the anger to surface and orchestrate her willingness to talk to her mother and receive professional counseling. The high from this achievement of getting her to talk was like no other I'd felt, and I wanted to do *more*. I was addicted to the passion to bring others to Christ. The reward surpassed anything I could receive physically or publicly.

In May, Victoria graduated and invited me to her graduation party. I was honored to be invited, and I knew her trainer would be there. I wanted to witness the dynamic between the two of them.

I don't know what I expected to see, because the party was like any other typical graduation barbecue. Her parents were inviting and friendly, her siblings interesting to talk to, and her trainer had as much right to be there as I did. I left chiding myself for passing judgment.

A week later, Victoria came by unexpectedly.

"I have pictures from prom and graduation I thought you'd like to see," she said.

Perfect timing. Seth and Ryan were down for a nap, and I was folding laundry. "Absolutely," I said. I waved her to the couch to sit. "You want something to drink? Water? A Coke?"

"I'm good, thanks."

I sat down next to her and flipped through the photo album. It didn't take long to see that her trainer was also present for the prom pictures. An uneasy feeling swirled in my stomach. "Your trainer sure does do a lot with your family."

She sat back, rigid. "Yeah. To be honest, I wish he didn't."

The next photo was of Victoria in her red, floor-length, sequined prom dress and her trainer with his arm around her waist. He smiled brightly and she grimaced.

I put the album down. "Why is it I don't get a good vibe when I see these pictures of you with your trainer?"

Her eyes bulged and she shifted positions. "Um, I don't know."

"It's just," I continued with caution, trying to find the right words. "Let me see . . . It's that he is so much older, he is divorced, and yet he is always around you."

She didn't blink, her eyes still as wide as half-dollars.

"Doesn't he train other girls? Is he hanging around them like this?"

She shrugged and finally looked away.

Silence filled the air for an excruciating few minutes. Somehow I knew if I remained still and quiet, more would be revealed.

The couch pillow that was wedged in her lap became her focal point. "Remember at the retreat, I asked you how do you know"—her voice shook—"if something is bad or not?"

"Yes."

"Well, I think I know. I just don't know what to do about it."

"Did he hurt you?"

She shook her head and pressed her face into the pillow. She shuddered and lifted her head. "That's the problem. It's complicated."

"Okay, then tell me what you think is bad."

She took a deep breath and wiped her eyes. "I can't believe I'm telling you this." She looked up, as if to God to ask permission. "I don't even know if it's any big deal."

I sat silent, afraid if I breathed too loud or even blinked, the moment for her to break free would pass.

"He has trained me since I was nine years old," she said. "When I was eleven, my mom sent me to tournaments with him, and we would stay in the same room. He was like an uncle or something; I really didn't think anything of it. We stayed in the same bed, and he never touched me or did anything to me."

The uneasiness in my stomach boiled as I listened.

"By the time I was in eighth grade, I was thirteen, and he was so much a part of our family that going away to tournaments was what we did. My mom would even come with us sometimes and stay in the same room. He would get two double beds then, and mom and I would share a bed."

She paused and picked at a loose thread on the pillow. Her face fell deeper into a grimace.

"But when she wasn't with us, he got closer. At first he wanted to cuddle, and then he kissed me. I was shocked and scared." She looked away. "But that's all he did. He said he loved me and always wanted to protect me. As I got older, more stuff happened, but he made it seem so natural, almost like we were going out or something."

Natural? I fumed inside and put my hand over my mouth because I didn't trust what might slip out.

"It's been like that ever since. It was weird at first. That's why I never dated. I felt like it would upset him. My first date was for prom." She sat back and sighed.

Lord, please give me the words to speak, I prayed.

"You know that's not normal, though, right?" I said. "I mean, you know whatever it is you guys did that was like a boyfriend and girlfriend wasn't okay for him to do? He had no right to put you in that position."

She kept her head leaned against the back of the couch but turned her face so she could see me. "That's where I get confused."

"No man has the right to touch, snuggle, cuddle, kiss, or whatever else with a *child*."

"But I was thirteen before he even started the cuddling. It didn't *feel* bad."

The urge to scream was so strong, I had to physically swallow it back. "You were a thirteen-year-old child who was put in a compromising position."

She doubled over, and the years of confusion, shame, frustration, anger and stolen innocence rushed forth like a tsunami. I reached over and put a hand on her back to reassure her. I resisted the natural instinct to hug her because I knew that in this situation, physical contact was not always welcomed.

"I don't think he is a bad person!" she said.

"It's okay. You're not to blame. Do you understand? I know you have feelings for him. How couldn't you? You spent most of your life with him. Something went haywire in his head, and instead of being your father figure, he looked to you to give him the affection he needed. It is a sickness."

She looked up at me then, her emerald eyes now a deep jade. "He treated me like I was his girlfriend. He got so mad when I told him I was going to prom"—her face puckered with distaste—"like I was betraying him."

"None of this is right. Trust me." I put a comforting hand on her arm. "You need to talk to someone who can help you. Have you told your mom?"

A slight snarl escaped her lips.

I was shocked.

"Honestly, I feel like my mom practically pushed us together." She broke into a torturous sob filled with anger. "Every time I tried to tell her I didn't feel comfortable going with him anymore, she insisted anyway. One time when I was fourteen, I tried to tell her about the kissing and she got mad at *me*! She told me I needed to quit pushing myself on him. That if he did anything else, it was my fault because I was asking for it."

A flashback of my grandfather saying the same thing about my mother and sister, that they asked for it, nearly sent me over the edge. I leaned in to grab her hand. "Victoria, this stops now. You will not stay with him anymore, right?"

She nodded.

"Do you want me to talk to your parents? Maybe I could talk to your dad?"

She shook her head. "Dad is clueless. He has so much going on at work, and my mom is always talking about my trainer like he is a god or something."

"What about counseling? If you asked your mom about getting counseling, would she ask why?"

"I don't know. Maybe?"

"You need to talk to someone about all of this."

"But I told you, and I feel *so* much better!"

I squeezed her hand. "And I'm glad you did, but I'm not a counselor, and if there is one thing I know, it is that when you've been through what you've been through, you need to be able to talk to someone in detail. Someone who is a professional and can guide you correctly."

"Well, I leave for college in two months. Maybe I could get counseling at school?"

Now what? I wondered. *What if she wouldn't tell anyone else? What do I do legally?*

She wasn't a minor anymore, so I knew I couldn't go without her permission to the authorities or her parents.

I certainly didn't want to lose her trust and have her stop talking to me. I knew she needed someone to confide in. I knew I needed someone when I was her age.

"I'm glad you told me," I finally said. "Thank you for trusting me."

CHAPTER 11

WEAK

Secure in your wickedness, you said, "No one sees me."

Your wisdom and your knowledge led you astray, and

you said in your heart, "I, and no one else!"

Isaiah 47:10

Another cry for help reverberated in my atmosphere, but it was too close for me to hear, even though it swept across the pages of my journal in black ink. A February entry said:

> *You know, Neal and I are arguing right now, and I can't even think straight. He's trying to tell me that my job is 24/7 raising the kids but that because I do CCE on Sunday nights and have a Bunco night once a month, I only do my job 12/7. The nerve!*
>
> *Men.*
>
> *Sometimes he can get me so riled up, I want to smack him with a new personality! One that is more sensitive and understanding. Maybe I am crazy . . . I just told him to leave.*

Ugh . . . now I'm pondering if I should be the one that breaks down and says I'm sorry. Maybe I should, but I'm sick of being told I'm crazy. Every time something happens, it is always "What did you do?" not "What happened?"

Man, he wears me down. He told me I was insecure but he makes me that way!

Right now I feel indifferent.

Neal and I had been married six years, and we'd been together for almost nine. We were comfortable and quick to push each other's buttons. My journal explained clearly the enemy's conniving ways of confusion and how slippery that slope truly can be—how in touch with God we can be and at the same time blinded by the enemy. In May, I wrote:

I certainly know that God is in control of my life, but I also know that sometimes it is hard to discern what is coming from him or is an evil trick of the enemy to throw me off course. So I pray. I know my destiny is to glorify God and His love and work in my writings. I feel it in the very marrow of my bones.

But in the meantime I'm trying to focus on Ryan and Seth. They are both adorable boys that I'm very proud of and they are both growing so fast. Ryan loves to sing and make believe. Maybe he'll be a writer or actor, too, one day? Seth loves to dance and wants me to read to him all of the time.

Neal and I are doing fine enough, but this is a tough time for us now. Maybe it's that seven-year itch? I love him just as much or even more than when we first met and fell in love, but it seems he is much more agitated these days, especially with me. One day we will be fine, but the next he'll say something rude or condescending and it's hurtful and I don't want to be around him. I want this time to pass so we can enjoy each other again.

Neal and I were strapped on a roller coaster, riding the emotional waves of a bipolar marriage. High above the financial issues, parenting disagreements, and consistency of sex (or lack thereof), we rose with our hands up, laughter in the air and smiles on our faces. Down, down, down we'd free-fall into the pit of anger, frustration, and pride, only to be thrust back up onto the next peak fast enough for the drops and falls to be pushed aside by the desperate need to feel happiness. At some point the ride was going to stop, but we didn't think about the fact it stops on the ground, where the pile of anger, frustration, and pride lingers.

This portion of the emotional roller coaster we were on felt like the climax of the ride, with one steep incline and dramatic free fall after another.

In July, I wrote:

I have to write about the awesome thing my husband did for me. We went to San Antonio for our anniversary weekend, and while we were gone, Neal had someone come in and clean the house. I mean—clean! It looks amazing. That's not all. He also paid to have the carpets cleaned, and, boy, did they need it. My neighbor bought flowers and put them on the table. It was so wonderful to come home to a super-clean house.

It is one of the sweetest, most special things Neal has ever done for me. I have a wonderful husband, and I love him dearly. I'm blessed.

The week following our return from San Antonio, I was invited by good friends of Neal's family to a bachelorette party in New Orleans. Neal made no fuss about me going, and even though we'd just had a break from the responsibility of the boys, I was happy to go along and have another.

In college, my girlfriends and I would go to New Orleans for the weekend and barhop from sunset to sunrise, fill up on beignets, and sleep through the next day until it was time to get up again and go at it one more time before we returned to school. We went often—until one time an unspeakable tragedy struck our sorority. A group of our girls went on an outing to New Orleans, but this time one girl trusted the wrong guys and was left with only a thread of life to sustain her. Repeatedly raped and beaten with her own clog shoe, it was a miracle she survived.

We stopped going to New Orleans after that incident.

Six years later, I thought about my sorority sister and considered backing out, but I was going to be with family. I would be safe.

Our group consisted of twelve women: the mother of the bride, the aunt of the bride, the bride, and six of her cousins and friends and myself. We took a short flight from Houston to New Orleans and were checked into our hotel by dinnertime Friday evening. The sun was already beginning to set, and a wave of deep bass and treble shook the closed merchants' windows as the nightclubs kicked into life along Bourbon Street.

The group took in a collective natural high partaking in New Orleans's special alcoholic drinks, the Hurricane and Grenade, Cajun **Étouffée,** and the type of laughter and joy that comes with a sloughing off of the daily grind. We christened our bride to be with her "Bachelorette" sachet and crown and entered into the crowds at the bars that spilled out of the doors and into the streets.

A few of the girls in our group ran over to a street vendor to buy more Hurricanes. I stood next to the mother and aunt and observed the crowd.

Where do I fit in? An unpleasant feeling nagged at my stomach. A year earlier, I would've been with the younger women, throwing back a few more of the fruit punch–flavored kerosene. Now I was older, possibly wiser, the mother of two boys, and trying to live a Christian life. What was I doing here?

The three of us older women stood in awkward silence as we watched the booty-bumping, body-humping throngs of people around us. The bride-to-be broke through the crowd and grabbed her mom's hand. "Come on!"

Her aunt and I followed.

Before we knew it, we were among the mix of hips and backsides gyrating to the latest R&B tunes. A quick-second song change, and the crowd went wild. It was a new line dance. The bride and her entourage slipped right into the steps as her mom and aunt struggled to keep up. They gave up after a few seconds and stood to the side. Quick to catch on, I hung in with the rest, and as the song played we clapped, stomped, and turned. I realized that a group of guys cozied up to the other ladies.

Another smooth transition, and the song moved right into a popular Top 40s hit. Song after song, the men stayed near the women, and after a few breaks and introductions, I found out the group was a bachelor party from up north.

The bachelor and our bachelorette had hit it off in a fun, friendly sort of way. The groups quickly meshed together, and the men became our protectors as we went from bar to bar for the night. Most of them were single, but there were a few married ones thrown in the mix.

By the end of the night, I was beat and sat out on a few songs, as did Sean, one of the married men from the other group. We tried to fill the awkwardness with small talk, but the music drowned out every other word. We gave up and laughed at the fools on the dance floor instead.

Around one or two in the morning, the bachelorette's mom, aunt, and I were fading fast. We couldn't hang with the others, so the young married man, Sean, and another guy from the bachelor's group offered to walk us back to the hotel. Away from the crowds, the bump of the bass, and people screaming to be heard because their eardrums were shot, we all took a moment to introduce ourselves.

Sean walked beside me. "We're all buddies from high school," he said. "Most of us went to college together too. Three of us in the group are married. Myself and Colby." He pointed to the other guy who was in conversation with the mom and aunt. "I'm the only one that has kids, though. I got married right after college."

I nodded and smiled politely. "How many kids do you have?"

"Three. Three boys all under the age of four. Colby's wife is expecting, and Matt just got married two months ago."

"I have two boys. Three and one. It feels weird to be here when I used to come when I was in college."

"Oh, yeah? I've never been here before. I don't think any of us have. We're from Michigan."

"I'm from Texas, the Houston area. But I went to college in East Texas, so it wasn't too far to drive. We used to come quite a bit."

"I bet you got in a lot of trouble here, huh?"

I smiled. "Tried not to. It is a dangerous place for girls, though." The memory of what happened to my friend made me shudder.

We were at our hotel.

"Thanks for walking us home," I said.

"Oh, yeah, no problem. Colby and I wanted to leave a while ago. I'm beat."

"Well, y'all have fun."

Sean smiled. "Y'all. I love the accent. I don't think I can get sick of hearing it."

I laughed and then felt uncomfortable. There was a moment of awkward silence, so I stepped closer to the women with me.

Later that morning, officially the next day, the bachelorette and her friends were still sleeping off the fun they had the night before. Our room, where the "married bunch" slept, walked to the French Quarter to Café Du Monde and munched on powdered beignets for breakfast. The moms bought a few dozen to take back with us, and as I waited for them to pay, I saw Sean, Colby, and a few of the other guys walk into the store.

I contemplated whether I should acknowledge them. We were essentially strangers that crossed paths in one of the craziest cities in the States.

The sun shone through the picture window and bounced off a stainless-steel napkin holder, blinding my sight. I squinted and stepped out of the glare.

"We run into y'all everywhere!" the aunt standing behind me called out.

I cringed. What if they don't want to keep up the friendly banter?

"Where is the rest of your crew?" Colby came over and set me at ease.

At least we didn't embarrass them too much.

"Still sleeping," I said. "What time did they get in, do *you* know?"

Sean walked up and stood next to me. "I think I heard Brad and the others roll in around four. They said something about hanging out with you guys this afternoon."

The eyebrows of the soon-to-be-bride's mother peaked. "Really?"

One of the other guys came up with a beignet in his hand and powdered sugar on his lips. "Yeah, we're gambling on that boat, I think."

I looked at the other two women and realized they were just as surprised as I was. "Okay, well I guess we'll see y'all this afternoon," I said.

"Y'all." Sean let the phrase roll off his tongue in a drawl. "Love it."

By afternoon, everyone was ready to go to make the most of the mini-vacation. We met up with the bachelor group at the gambling boat. I dreaded going there, not because I didn't like to gamble but because I didn't have the funds to blow. Gambling wasn't supposed to be a part of the trip, but because most of the girls enjoyed the attention of other guys in the group, our plans had changed.

I dragged my feet once we were at the pier. I called Neal to see how Ryan and Seth were doing, and when I got off the phone I saw Sean lingering as well, talking on his cell phone. I waited for him to finish.

"Calling home too?" I asked.

"Yeah, the little guys are giving my wife trouble." He laughed. "She played it cool now, but I know I'll get it when I get back."

I laughed because I knew I probably wouldn't be too happy to have Neal out with the guys in New Orleans. It was a double standard, and I blushed, recognizing the fact.

"You guys are all the same," he said.

"Well, I mean you have three kids. I can imagine how hard it is to be left alone with them all weekend."

"Why aren't you going on the boat?"

I shrugged. "I'm going, I guess. I don't really have any money to gamble."

He leaned over the metal railing that kept us from pitching over the cement embankment into the canal. "Yeah, I'm broke too."

There was something about his mannerism that seemed familiar. He reminded me of one of my best guy friends in college. The one who in many ways saved me from myself when I was at my most destructive.

Sean wasn't a guy who would drive the girls to clamor to get his attention, but he wasn't homely either. He was about an inch taller than me, had dark features and a friendly smile, and wore the efforts of his wife's cooking well. His demeanor was at ease, and I felt safe standing next to him.

"Well, don't feel like you have to hang out here with me," I said. "I'll go in and find everyone."

He laughed. "Trust me, the way my guys play, they'll be back out in thirty minutes."

I laughed.

"There are some benches over there. Let's sit down and wait it out."

We sat down on the bench, and I asked him questions about his wife and kids. He pulled out pictures in his wallet, and I showed him a tiny photo album of pictures I kept in my purse of Neal and the boys.

"My oldest is in pre-K3 at a Catholic school," I said.

"You're Catholic?"

"Yeah. Yes, I am." It felt good to claim it and mean it.

"So am I. Well, I was brought up Catholic. My wife, too, but we don't really go anymore. I attended Catholic schools all my life, though."

"I stopped going for a while, too, but recently I've had a change of heart . . . I guess you could call it that."

"What do you mean?"

I divulged a few simple details of the struggle I had finding faith and figuring out what it meant. I didn't want him to know too much about my dark past and what led me to the place of anger and despair.

He seemed intrigued, and time passed quickly before a cluster of his friends mixed with the girls in my group walked off the boat.

I stopped in midsentence, feeling exposed and vulnerable. *Why are you telling this stranger your most personal business?* I chastised myself.

"Have you guys been sitting out here this whole time?" one of the girls from my group asked in disbelief.

"Yeah," said one of Sean's friends, hitting him on the shoulder. "Sean here is a tightwad. It takes a lot for him to part with his money."

Sean smiled and took a mock swing at his buddy. "So why don't you tell me how much you're down, huh? One hundred dollars? Two hundred?"

The guy threw up his hands and backed away from Sean. "Ok, okay . . . just playin'."

I was curious. "How much *did* you lose?"

The guy mumbled something under his breath.

Sean laughed and jumped up to tackle him. "What was that? Five hundred dollars?"

"You lost five hundred?" I was shocked. I stood with the other girls and could tell we all thought the same thing: *Do you know what I could do with five hundred dollars?*

By this time, the rest of our groups emerged from the boat and the bachelor and bachelorette made plans for the two groups to meet up after we went our separate ways for dinner. They had agreed to hang out with us for the rest of the night to keep both groups safe.

Before the groups split, Sean walked over to me. "Hey, I want to hear the rest of your story later. You got my attention."

I did? I smiled, proud. It felt *good* telling him about what God had done in my life. I could sense he was as lost as I was. It was invigorating to be able to help someone else see the light and know God's love.

But the rest of the story would have to wait until the wee hours of the next morning.

The groups converged after dinner and hopped from one club to the next. We learned every new hip line dance, like the Macarena and Cha Cha Slide, to old dance moves, like the Tootsee Roll, Da Dip, and the Humpty Dance. I hadn't danced that much since college, and with every new move, dip, and shake I felt all of my inhibitions fall to the dance floor.

It was liberating to dance and cut up with this group of women of all ages and to have a group of guys to dance with and not feel the pressure of any mixed signals. We were all out to have a good time and enjoy the culture of New Orleans.

But age won out, and the three of us who were the oldest deflated once we passed midnight into the early morning hours. We made our plans to catch a taxi home and let the other girls continue on with their last night.

Sean walked up to us. "Hey, I'll take you guys back. You don't need to get a taxi."

"You'd do that for us?" The ladies gushed over his chivalry. I secretly celebrated the fact he saw something in me that made him want to know more about my faith. I was on a mission and wasn't going to let God down.

Careful not to step across the blurred lines of appropriate and inappropriate discussion between two married people, I sat in the hallway of the hotel, right outside the room I shared with the two other women. Sean sat across from me and leaned against the opposite wall.

Neal jokes that I can meet people and in five minutes have learned their life stories and manage to memorize their social security numbers. He isn't too far off. I know he is apologizing to others for my nosiness when he says this, but I'd like to think it's being in tune to the details.

I didn't jump right into my conversion story with Sean. I wanted to know more about him before I tried to push God and our Catholic faith.

"Tell me more about your wife and kids," I said.

"Stacey and I met in high school. We've been dating since we were fifteen."

"Fifteen? Wow, that's kind of cool."

He shrugged his shoulders. "Yeah, it is. We broke up a few times and tried dating other people in college, but somehow we always came back together. Then she got pregnant and . . . " He shrugged his shoulders and lifted his hands in surrender. "We got married."

"I got married young." I laughed and snorted. Embarrassed, I laughed harder. "Sorry, I do that sometimes. I'm laughing because it's not like I'm old. I'm only twenty-eight."

"Really? I'm younger than you?" He smiled.

"What? You *are*?"

"Yeah, I'm only twenty-six. Just *turned* twenty-six. You're an old woman."

"Oh, jeez, thanks."

We both laughed.

I played with my wedding ring. "Well, I guess if I'm older, then I'm wiser."

"I'd say so."

His words hung in the air. Embarrassed, I looked away.

"Earlier you were telling me what made you go back to church," he said. "Was your family really strict in the faith when you were growing up?"

With an ease that surprised me, I opened up about my family with its issues, but I wasn't about to talk about anything deeply personal, like the rapes.

Sean stretched his legs out. "My family was pretty normal. We went to Mass every Sunday, and my parents rarely fought. I did my share of stupid things in high school, but other than that life was boring. I didn't have to go to CCE classes because we got religion in school."

"What did your parents do when they found out Stacey was pregnant? That had to have shaken things up a bit."

He looked up and past me to a memory in his mind and laughed. "Yeah, you could say that. Our parents made sure we got married quick so it wasn't an *issue*." He punctuated his sentence with his fingers, framing the words in quotes.

"Stacey and I fight all the time." He bent his head and traced the pattern on the carpet with his finger. "She isn't happy."

Now it was personal. *Danger! Danger!* My heart rate escalated. Here was the line I didn't want to cross. *Bring it back to God.*

"Have you ever thought of going back to church?"

"Right. Like that will cure everything."

"No." On impulse I reached out and touched his arm, then snapping my hand back as if I touched a hot coal. "Well, yes." I fumbled with my words. "I mean, I think it does. I mean, my husband is like you and doesn't want to really do as much as I do with the church, but . . . "

The elevators came to life, and the girls stumbled out. The bride-to-be looked at me and cocked her head to the side, as if to say something but thought better of it.

I scrambled to my feet. No one said a word, and the four of them fell into their room, passing out wherever they landed.

Sean and I looked at each other and laughed.

"I guess my crew is back at the hotel too," he said.

"I better get some sleep. We have an early flight tomorrow."

"Today, you mean."

"Well . . . " I hesitated, not quite sure how to say goodbye. "It was good getting to know you. Good luck with everything."

An awkward moment passed where I had a sense of regret. But regret for what? I turned and let myself into the room.

Four hours later, my group was packed and wheeling bags out to the waiting car service. All of the young men from the bachelor group were waiting outside, including Sean.

"We thought we'd say goodbye," the bachelor offered. I turned in time to see the bride-to-be's mother and aunt exchange a curious look between them.

"Hey." Sean walked up and handed me a slip of paper. "Here is my e-mail. I want to keep in touch. Write yours down on this." He handed me a notepad from his hotel.

My heart fluttered with the flattery, and I could feel heat rise to my cheeks. What was wrong with me? It was just an e-mail. But I knew deep inside I enjoyed a man's approval, no matter who or how old. It was a curse—the need to be accepted and desired by men.

"Thanks." I wrote down my e-mail address. "Y'all be safe."

He smiled. "*Y'all*," he mimicked. "I'll miss that."

The flutter increased, and I turned to get in the car before he could see my red face. All the way to the airport, I replayed our conversation from the night before in my mind, trying to figure out why I felt like a schoolgirl who had been given a note by the boy she had a crush on. Did I flirt? I didn't recall saying anything that wasn't appropriate or even looking at him in that way.

However, it felt good to be noticed, to be liked, to appear normal when I struggled every day with Neal to *be* normal for him. Through no fault of his own, he was too close. He knew my brokenness and my inability to perform as I felt a wife should. We had worn each other down with our issues. With Neal I felt consistently inadequate, not because Neal knew how to push my buttons of insecurity to cause this feeling but because I had a vision of what I felt like normal *should* look like.

The simple and innocent night spent talking with Sean was a reprieve. There had been no expectation of anything because of the obvious boundary of our marriages, and he knew nothing of my past. As far as Sean knew, other than my family issues, I had it all together.

Spent and ready for me to come home, Neal greeted me at the door with Seth. I gave him a big hug and kiss, and he received it with trepidation. I wasn't the one to instigate affection; I withdrew from affection. Something in the exchange with Sean helped me to feel a taste of confidence in myself again.

I took Seth into my arms and felt he needed a diaper change. By the time I was done, I went back into the living room to tell Neal all about the weekend, but he was already gone. I sighed. It was the typical game. I was gone for two and a half days, so now it was his turn to get out and relieve some steam.

Despite the few hours of sleep, my blood flowed. I cleaned the house while the kids napped, played trains with Ryan, and when he was preoccupied watching a video, I checked e-mail.

The first e-mail I noticed was the last received. An e-mail from Sean. My heart pounded.

What am I doing? I scolded myself for reacting to the attention. It was a weakness I had noticed over the years— receiving attention from men. Later in counseling, I would find out this is a common behavior for survivors of abuse. Of course, I didn't realize this at the time and just assumed it stemmed from years of watching my sister flirt with her boyfriends. Watching it caused feelings within me that as a child I couldn't understand but it felt good. If someone of the opposite sex looked at me as if I was desirable, then it made me feel those same feelings.

I brushed the feeling away like an annoying gnat and opened the e-mail.

The gut of the e-mail was both shocking and secretly pleasing:

I enjoyed our conversation and I hope you don't take offense to this, but I can't stop thinking about you. I know it's inappropriate. I don't mean any harm, and I don't expect anything, but I had to tell you. I know you might be offended, and if so, I'm sorry. I can't help but want to know more about you and about our Catholic faith. Can we still talk? As friends?

And there it was. The line was obliterated. The apple dangled from the forbidden tree. Like a cartoon character, I imagined a little devil, pitchfork and all, popping up on my left shoulder and a little angel, Bible in hand, on my right.

"He is thinking about you," the devil schemed. "You matter to him."

"Delete the e-mail. Don't respond. This is a test," the angel pleaded.

"It's not that big of a deal. You're making what he wrote into something more than it is. He wants to know more about his faith. You're helping him," the devil said convincingly.

"It isn't fair to Neal to e-mail or talk to another man. It's not the attention you want," the angel's voice said, getting smaller.

"Tell Neal about Sean. It's not that big of a deal. Neal trusts you, and what could it hurt? The guy lives states away."

The devil won.

I wrote back:

Hey, Sean. It was good to meet you as well. It's always fun getting to know other people. Any time you have a question, you're welcome to ask.

Later, when Neal came home from hanging out with his friends, we sat in bed and talked about the weekend in New Orleans. I was truthful and told him about the bachelor party that we hung out with and the conversation I picked up with Sean. If it bothered Neal, he didn't show it. Instead we made up for lost intimate time while I was gone.

I allowed my mind to enter into a world where Neal didn't know all of the brokenness about me, and it gave me a boost. My senses were awakened, as if a key had unlocked the door to my inhibitions. I felt freer, more confident. I had beaten myself down with Neal over the years and convinced myself that I could not live up to what he deserved because of all of the triggers. During sex, I could not speak or make a sound. I couldn't be touched in certain ways or places; even the smell of our union at times made me cringe. I felt unsure and unable to be who he deserved.

But maybe I'd found a way.

The following week, Sean and I e-mailed on a daily basis. Within the week, we exchanged IMs, and he messaged me first thing in the morning. Nothing was written that broke a marital vow. It was everything else that created the fall.

Tormented by this new friendship and whether or not it was "of God" or a door for the enemy to slip in, I went to my journal and prayed for God to reveal a purpose of our friendship. I wrote:

Sean and I talk a lot about spirituality and religion. Today he asked me to tell him what makes me "so faithful." I had to laugh because I remember not long ago asking what faith was and how to get it. He wanted me to tell him what made me so sure. So I did, and it was awesome! I told him that no matter what I said, it would ultimately be up to him to get a true understanding or belief. I continued to give him my basic testimony, and he listened. I mean, really listened. When it was all said and done (this is what I'll cherish forever and I totally lift it up to God), he got real serious and said, "In all my life, not from my grandparents, my parents, or going to Catholic schools and church on Sunday, have I ever had faith explained to me in such a way that makes sense as you have explained it to me today."

Praise God. I asked God to speak through me, and He did. What an awesome feeling. I pray Sean looks into this more. If I could reach people like this all the time, my life would be so full and blissfully high. I'm so blessed. Thank you, God!

I was hooked. Sean was a project, someone I could save, whereas Neal wanted nothing to do with my newly found vigor for evangelization.

When Neal got home from work, I'd venture to have the same discussions, but he often met me with a blank stare or a simple, "That's interesting."

It was a slow fade, but one that had been coming on for awhile. Neal and I were not on the same page. We fought daily about the simplest of issues—who did more, who cared more, who said something more hurtful or demeaning than the other. I didn't feel appreciated, respected, or supported. He didn't feel appreciated, respected, or supported. We were at an impasse.

The thrill of knowing someone who knew nothing about me made things better with Neal, but I could no longer carry that over into my existing relationship. The little devil on my shoulder convinced me maybe Neal hadn't been right for me from the beginning.

Neal would come home and surpass me to give his attention to the boys and then head out to be with his friends. *He doesn't love me as I deserve,* I'd fume inside. *Or at all.*

Weeks turned into a month, and my friendship with Sean was more like a long-distance relationship. We had regular times to talk on a daily basis. We dove into one another's life, what was going on with our kids, what our spouses were doing or saying that caused us both to feel inadequate and displeased.

We spoke less and less of faith and focused more on ourselves—our selfish needs and desires. When I ventured a daydream about living a different life, the angel groped her way through the fog. "What are you doing? You're playing with fire."

Ryan was in preschool and Seth was eighteen months old when I received an invitation for a new Bible study taking place at a friend's home.

"What study is it?" I asked, but it didn't matter. I knew I needed something to save me from myself.

"It's on spiritual warfare."

My heart pounded through my chest as I choked back the guilt and tears. "Yes, I'll be there," I said. God had perfect timing.

The invitation itself served as a personal wake-up call. If anyone should recognize the enemy's ways, it should be me, but I was caught up in the web of lies. I avoided Sean's routine phone call and ignored his IMs.

"He cares about you," the devil on my shoulder said, wiping away my tears of anguish and confusion with more lies. "He doesn't understand why you won't talk to him. At least give him an explanation."

Unable to withstand the guilt of hurting anyone, I gave in and called. Sean understood what we had was nothing beyond a fantasy life that was based on deceptive illusion. But the enemy was smart and conniving, and even in our understanding we couldn't stop the simple principle of caring for one another.

The Bible study began, and every word of every paragraph leapt off the page like alarm bells. "Get out of his grasp!" they cried. "Wake up to his lies!" they screamed. "Fight back!" they wailed.

I wept in the shower. *God, help me.*

I wanted my marriage to be a good marriage. I wanted with Neal what we had in the beginning and not what we'd become—like roommates in the same home. The grips of the enemy had tightened around me, but this time I could taste, smell, and see the pit that had claimed my life for years. I fought back with every ounce of strength I could muster, and when I didn't have enough, Christ stood in the gaps.

In January, I wrote in my journal:

> *I am horrified that I haven't journaled in five months. I guess it shows the turmoil I've been facing: I don't even want to write my true thoughts down when I'm not sure of how I feel about them myself.*
>
> *I don't talk to Sean as much anymore. I think God needed me to speak to him and then let it go, but the enemy snuck in and put me to the test. I'd like to think I passed. Sean and I check in every now and then to see how our families are doing, but that's it. I do believe he was a blessing meant to open my eyes in my own marriage. I do thank God for that. If I take a look back at the past year, it makes me sad, proud, and blessed. This year was full of some of the most challenging and difficult experiences in my life, even more so than the rapes, because they were spiritual attacks. But I think it*

has also made it the most rewarding. God has granted me wisdom through these tests, and that humbles me.

Neal and I suffered this year, but we are on the climb back up . . . at the moment. We have a long way to go. There are so many obstacles and variables in our way. I nearly left Neal two months ago. It's not that I really felt like we were over. But I had reached my breaking point, and I believe he had too. But we stopped ourselves from separating and resolved to get over this big bump together. We went to counseling with our parish priest, Fr. Ken, because he didn't know either of us, which felt unbiased and was helpful. I went back to personal counseling to deal with the sex/lack-of-desire issue, and it has helped, but I think Neal is a little beyond being compliant in "helping" me "get better." Get better . . . hmm . . . to be honest, I'm not sure I can. And why is it that it's always my issue or my fault? Argh . . . I guess that's my hang-up in all of this.

I do feel for Neal. For so many years he has felt shunned and inadequate. I'd take it all back if I could. But that's not how God created the world. We are to move forward, and it's my future that I can control (with God holding the reins, of course).

What is interesting and ironic is that through some strange (and not really wanted) occurrences, I have come to realize I am a sexual person who is wanted and can desire. So, I do look forward to seeing what might be of this "new" me.

At the moment Neal and I are selling our home to move to a new area. I pray this is in God's will for us. I have learned enough to know it's God's will I desire above all. This next year will be better. I feel it.

"I think I'm ready to move."

Neal had come home with the idea one evening after visiting a co-worker's home who lived in another suburb of Houston, forty-five minutes north of where we currently lived. "There is something about this place that tells me you'll never want to leave."

Stunned into silence, I stared at my husband, who had refused the idea of moving away from what was comfortable. Why the sudden change of heart? Then I realized it didn't matter. This was our chance to start over.

The move happened within nine months, and even though the proximity of location made no difference to the distance I had between Sean and me, I allowed it to be the final good-bye to what never would be or ever should have been.

Before we moved, I found the courage to confess my sin.

"Tell your husband the truth, and go on a married couples' retreat," the priest directed as my penance.

Turns out God had more in store for us before we could make that happen.

CHAPTER 12

A NEW START

"For I know well the plans I have in mind for you—oracle of the

LORD*—plans for your welfare and not for woe,*

so as to give you a future of hope."

Jeremiah 29:11

Either take my life or do something with it!

I had challenged God with my face pressed into synthetic carpet. Two years later, close to the exact day, living in a new town and starting over, with Neal and me on the same page of knowing not a single soul in the area, God cashed in.

The boys and I walked out of our new parish's Family Life Center. They were in the summer Mother's Day Out program. A woman I vaguely recognized met me in front of the doors.

"Shannon Deitz?" she asked.

Seth hung from one hand, dragging behind, still tired from the nap I'd disturbed, while Ryan ran ahead, threatening to run into the middle of the street. I stopped to acknowledge the woman, but Ryan ran ahead.

"Ryan Deitz! Stop right there."

Ryan stopped before his feet touched the parking lot.

The woman gasped.

"Sorry, I said."

I picked Seth up, swung him onto my hip, and ran after Ryan, who laughed and ran in the opposite direction, past me and toward the Family Life Center doors. I reached out to grab him but only grazed his shoulder with the tips of my fingers.

Ryan squealed in delight and unknowingly ran right into the woman's arms.

"Hey there, little man," she said.

Ryan's eyes got big, and he wiggled free to run back to me.

With both boys in my grasp I looked at the woman. "I'm sorry."

"Oh, my son is three years old too." She smiled. "Remember me—Patricia Vincent? I gave you the tour of the school."

Embarrassed I had forgotten so easily when it had only been four months since I'd taken the tour, I laughed. "Yes, yes, of course. I know Ryan looks forward to pre-K4."

Ryan pressed his nose on the backside of my leg to hide.

"Well, I was actually looking for you," she said. "Didn't you say you had experience working with teens when you were in Deer Park?"

I nodded, hesitant, unsure if I *had* said anything.

Her smile widened. "Oh, good! I thought that was you. I couldn't quite remember who it was, but for some reason your name kept coming to mind. Our parish has a part-time youth ministry position open, and I told them about you."

My heart fluttered. Being in youth ministry was a call I *wanted* to have but knew with my past mistakes, especially having come off of what was undoubtedly an emotional affair and the fact that my kids were still young, that it would be a dream for the future.

My cheeks blazed with the shame. I turned my head, thinking, *I'm a sinner. You don't want me.*

"Oh, I wouldn't say I had that much experience," I said.

She smiled and pressed forward. "I don't know what it is, Shannon, but I think you should at least talk to Carole, our full-time youth minister, and Henry, the faith formation director. They are in the office right now." She pointed to a glass door that was to the right of the Family Life Center. "I can introduce you and then watch the boys while you talk to them."

She didn't wait for my excuse. She quickly turned and walked to the glass door, opening it before I had a chance to say a word. "That young woman is out here that I was telling y'all about," I could hear her say. "Do y'all want to talk to her now? I can watch her boys while you do that."

With a flick of her manicured hand, she waved me into the office.

"This is Shannon Deitz." She grabbed my hand to pull me through the door and past her, then stepped closer to me and took Seth from my arms. "I'll keep the boys outside while y'all talk."

The group inside sat at a round table in the middle of the office space. I shook hands with Paula, the head of catechesis, along with Carole, the youth minister, and Henry, the head of faith formation. They looked at me, and everyone seemed prepared and ready for this impromptu interview except me.

There was no time to think or object. The group around the table asked questions about the volunteer work I'd done with the youth and about my education. I spoke about the teens, the CCE class I co-taught, and the Confirmation retreats. As promised, the visit was quick, and I was left with an invitation to apply for the part-time youth ministry position. The position was not a lot of money, but it was enough to help us pay a bill or two for the month.

At home, I agonized about the chance meeting. I was torn inside because I had made a promise to God that if He would get me out of the sticky situation with Sean and back on the right track, I would do whatever it took to be a good mother and devoted wife. Plus, now that Ryan was beginning preschool in the upcoming school year and Seth would be in Mother's Day Out, I was preparing to take the extra time to write. If I took the part-time youth minister position, I would have no time to write.

Snuggled in my grandmother's antique wingback chair in my bedroom, I took out my prayer journal and flipped to a page I recalled writing a few months before we made our final move:

If I am to get a job or become a writer or even work for the church (or both), please confirm this for me, Lord! How am I to help our household financially and follow Your will?

I smiled and felt an overwhelming sense of peace cover me like a warm blanket. The journal was now on its last few empty pages, and I knew this was the last prayer I needed to offer up to complete this journey and begin a new one. I turned to a blank page and wrote:

Lord, the strangest thing happened today, which only means it was of You. So, please know I don't take this possible position as a part-time youth minister lightly. I never thought all of this would happen so soon. I assumed the kids would be older and in school. But this is perfect. It is part-time and enough money to help with some of the bills. I don't see how Neal could say no. But, Lord, I'll be honest. I was hoping to have the chance to write more. If you want me to do this job and be able to focus on ministry and my family, then please take away this desire to write.

I finished writing in the journal, making sure to include prayers for the boys, Neal, and other people who had asked for prayers.

The boys were getting up from their naps and I could hear them rustling around in the playroom upstairs when the phone rang.

"Hello?" I said.

"Shannon Deitz, please."

"This is she." I had my finger on the END button, certain it was a telemarketer.

"Mrs. Deitz, I'm the senior editor at ABC Publishing, and we have been considering your manuscript, *Corner of My Mind*, for quite some time."

My grip tightened around the receiver, and I froze in place. "Yes?"

"Well, we enjoy the manuscript and were considering it for publication, but we have also been struggling with some financial difficulties, which is what has kept us from making a decision. Unfortunately, we are not able to continue and will have to send back the manuscript. Of course we'll offer you a recommendation."

Disappointment and anticipation collided, leaving me speechless.

"I'm very sorry we are not able to offer you a contract at this time."

I smiled despite the obvious disappointment. There was my answer, as clear as day. "Thank you for calling," I said.

When I hung up, the disappointment was gone. I asked God to take away the desire to write so I could focus on what He wanted me to do. For me, this phone call was God telling me, *You are a good writer and you will write, but not right now.*

My answer was clear. The anxiety was gone, replaced by the anticipation and excitement of what being involved in youth ministry could bring.

Once I got involved in youth ministry, it took over my life, and though I was still there for the kids to take them to preschool and pick up at the end of the day, I was gone at least one, if not two or three, nights a week and every other weekend. And if I wasn't at the office or doing a youth program, then I was on the phone with a teenager or parent, helping them deal with an issue. The part-time aspect of the position lasted merely a few months before I was asked to take on the position full time.

Neal was on board in the beginning because it meant I would receive a full-time salary—a little less than a private school teacher brings in, but it was enough to make life a little easier on us financially. Plus, I worked where the kids were in Mother's Day Out and preschool, so it was convenient and offered the best of all worlds.

What Neal and I didn't anticipate was how much of myself I would pour into the job, leaving little to give when I got home.

I stood before Neal and saw the resignation in his eyes, and it felt like our world was about to implode.

"What's going on with us, Shannon?" Neal sat on our couch in the living room and looked up at me with a mixture of disdain and confusion. "We're like roommates living in the same house."

I stood before him with my hands on my hips, the defensive stance I often took when we were in one of our heated battles. These days it seemed we were in a battle of wills daily. Gone was the bliss of the roller coaster. At least it had peaks. We'd come to the end of our ride, and neither of us wanted to be the first to exit.

He was right. We weren't living as a married couple.

"You could care less to be with me," he said with resignation in his voice. "I don't think you care about our sex life at all."

My teeth clenched. Sex. Ugh.

"Then let's go to counseling," I said.

Even though the fear of losing him sent alarms through every nerve in my body, it still didn't cancel out the hurt I felt by the original argument. It all came down to sex.

Curse the evil serpent in the Garden of Eden. If Adam and Eve could have lived blissfully, avoiding the fruit of the forbidden tree, we wouldn't have the issue of how often sex happened, who initiated it, and every emotional trigger in between. Of course, it wasn't really about sex. Sex was the easy fight to have. The underlying issue was much deeper and more complex.

Neal rolled his eyes. "We don't need to go talk to some stranger. *You* might need counseling, but I don't."

"You are such a jerk!"

I regretted it the minute it erupted, because not only did I work diligently to not yell anymore, it was like the curse of any bad habit: once you give in, you can't stop.

Even as we piled on the useless words, one on top of the other, I felt my spirit cry out. *What are you doing? Stop! Stop right now!*

My resolve broke. I cried. The fight was over.

God, I prayed in my journal, *You have shown me how valuable it is to be patient for Your time, because You'll know when I'm ready to be an example of Your light and love to others, but right now I realize it's not time. It's not time because I can't get my own marriage right. It's not just me who has to be ready to do whatever it is You are calling me to. It is Neal too! We have to be one another's rock to hold on to, and we'll have to share the same convictions, and I'm not sure we are there right now.*

Another eye-awakening You have given me, Lord, is what is keeping me from feeling love, desire, and the passion I long to have in my marriage. It is so simple. I'm afraid to love. I love—I love my husband and boys—but it's a guarded love. I now see this. It's why I get testy and short and why I back off at times. My heart literally puts up a wall, because if I were to give 100 percent of me to love them, then how would I recover if I were to lose one of them? Or if I were to be hurt by them? I'm keeping defenses up, and it is silly!

Lord, tear down this wall I've built up around myself. Help me to love—to love like You want me to love. I have got to let go and allow You to lead me and to do as You command. LOVE.

As if on cue, God orchestrated a conversation between me and another woman who worked at the parish who brought up the fact that she and her husband were going through marital counseling. Without hesitation, I obtained the number for the counselor and made an appointment.

I chose a peaceful evening to bring up the appointment to Neal. My moment of surrender to God only two years before came back to me like a cup of cold water splashed in my face. *Offer it up.*

"Neal, I was thinking, and you're right. I do need counseling, so I made an appointment with a counselor someone at work told me about."

I had him at *You were right*, so I continued. "But I was hoping you would come with me to this first visit so you could help explain what it is I need to work on."

To Neal's credit, he has not been one to back away from doing what was needed to help me in my recovery. Before we were married he attended counseling with me, and we'd been to see Fr. Ken, so for him this wouldn't be any different.

I sat on the couch, Neal sat on the chair next to the couch, and the therapist sat in her desk chair, positioned in front of us, with a yellow notepad balanced on her lap.

"I'm not a priority for Shannon," Neal said.

My stomach fell. I couldn't argue my way out of this one.

The therapist scribbled on her notepad and then looked in my direction. "When you hear Neal say this, what does this mean to you?" she asked.

My lips quivered and my throat tightened. I shrugged and tried to swallow. "That he doesn't feel like I put him first or maybe that I don't even care."

"Is that how you feel, Neal?"

He was apathetic. I could sense it in his slight slouch and poker face. "Yeah, pretty much."

I found my voice. "I do care. There is a lot of pressure, and I guess it's easier to get lost in work or the kids."

"What do you mean by pressure?" she asked.

Neal sat up in his chair and turned to look at me.

I knew if I said what I felt, it would hurt Neal, and I was certain he wouldn't understand. My face burned with shame. "I know I don't give Neal what he needs, and when I'm at work I feel good about what I'm doing. It's easier to be at work, where I feel like I'm not a failure, than it is to be at home and know I can't live up to what Neal feels is normal."

Neal's face crunched up in disgust. "Why do you say that? I don't make you do anything you don't want to do, and I don't ever tell you I expect something from you."

"You say that, but you do. We can't be intimate without it having to lead to sex."

"What? That's ridiculous. I don't even ask for it any-more because you make me feel worse—like I'm putting you out."

"Well, it's because I feel like we can't even hold hands or sit next to each other without you thinking it should lead to sex!"

"You don't want me." He looked dejected and turned to the therapist. "She doesn't desire me. To be honest, I'm sick of trying, only to get rejected and made to feel like I'm some bad guy for wanting to be with her."

His words stung like salt on a fresh wound. I wanted to interject and tell him he was being ridiculous, but he was right. I loved him and I found him very attractive, but there was a rock-solid mental block when it came to feeling *desire*.

"I'm sorry," I said, "but it's hard when you make comments on how I'm not keeping up with some quota." It felt good to admit this out loud. "And you joke about it in front of your friends, but it's not funny."

His eyes widened. "I don't joke about it."

"Yes, you do. You say things that refer to the fact that I'd rather not have sex or how you never get it or how mistreated you are . . . or even how I would never be like some sex-crazed person."

"Well, it's true. That's not a joke."

"But it hurts when you talk about it in front of your friends." How could he not see that?

For the hour we were in her office, the therapist spent most of it clarifying our emotions to one another. We peeled back layers, which left us raw and exposed.

In the end, she asked if we would be willing to partake in some healing homework. She suggested I could use personal therapy to deal with some issues that I hadn't touched upon in past counseling.

Knowing the cause was still in my court, Neal leaned in with interest. Right away I felt frustrated, because I didn't want Neal to be fooled by the thought I could be fixed and no longer have these issues.

"What is the project and then I'll tell you if I think it's doable," Neal asked.

"I think you have an issue with boundaries." She looked me right in the eye. "You're afraid to say no because you never had the freedom to before without it leading to a loss of some kind. Am I close?"

Hearing her say this aloud was as if the numbness from a third-degree burn had worn off, and I could feel the excruciating pain for the first time. I *was* too afraid to say no, but I didn't acknowledge it. It was more of an internal defense that led to my frustration during intimate moments, *especially* if I wasn't close to being in the mood.

I nodded.

Neal interrupted. "You can say no to me."

"Wait a second," the therapist intervened. "You hear this and think it is such an easy fix to the problem—"Just say no"—but this is a deeper issue with Shannon. She needs to feel comfortable being able to be near you and not feel as if she has to deliver sexually. She needs to feel a sense of safety and comfort with you so she can create these healthy boundaries and be able to receive the feelings of desire without them triggering a defensive reaction."

Neal looked as if he could cry, which made me want to cry harder. This was as hard on him as it was on me.

"I'll do whatever it is she needs," he said.

"What I'd like to propose is that you guys start all over again intimately, and I want Shannon to be in control of what pace you guys move."

Neal and I looked at each other with eyebrows raised.

"In this first phase, I don't want you to touch, kiss, or have sex. I want you to be around each other and talk like you normally do, but no touching. She needs to know you are here for her even without the sexual intimacy. I need Shannon to be in the driver's seat on this."

"Ugh, she's *always* in the driver's seat." Neal looked at me and gave a reassuring smile.

A sense of panic swirled in the pit of my stomach. I understood the concept of this homework, but it terrified me to be in that position.

"How long should we do this?" I asked.

"Until you feel like you want to hold his hand. Just hold his hand, nothing else."

"Hold his hand? Come on." The panic moved up to my chest. "I like to hold Neal's hand." I looked over at him. He wouldn't look at me. The tightening in my chest mirrored the pain he had to be feeling.

"I realize it seems extreme, but the two of you need to treat this as a chance to push the reset button. Go out on dates. Get to know each other again. How long have you been married?"

"Eight years," we answered in unison.

"And I'm sure you dated for a year or two before you got married?"

I nodded.

"Neal, how are you feeling about this homework?"

He shrugged. "I don't know. To be honest, I wouldn't be surprised if we never get past this first step."

So this is what it had come to. I had pushed my husband to the edge, and now he felt as if I didn't even want to be near him, let alone hold his hand. Unable to get a word past the lump in my throat, I looked to the therapist, pleading with my eyes to help save this ship we were sinking fast.

She smiled. "Shannon, how do *you* feel about this homework?"

"I feel like I want to quit it already, like I'm going to lose him." I faced Neal. "I *do* want to hold your hand, and I *do* want to be with you. *I don't know why it is so hard.*" The tears wouldn't stop.

Within seconds, Neal was on the couch beside me, wrapping me in an embrace. "Hey, I'm not going anywhere. I know you love me, and I'll do whatever we need to do."

I cried harder. It felt like Neal always gave in and gave up for me. "I'm sorry."

The therapist interjected. "No, don't apologize. Accept the love he is showing you and recognize you *deserve* it."

I slumped into Neal's embrace, knowing that it might be a little while before I felt his arms around me again. I wrangled my emotions back enough to sit up and finish the session.

"So, are we all in agreement?" the therapist asked. "For as long as you need, Shannon, you'll call the shots on when you can hold hands, and that's it. If that takes a week, two weeks, or even a month, then that's what it takes. Once you feel like you desire and want to hold Neal's hand, then we'll discuss what the next step is."

We nodded in agreement. Before leaving, we set up our appointment for the following week, and I made an appointment to see her one on one before our next couple's session.

The next day, I did not desire to hold Neal's hand. But there wasn't a chance to do it even if I had desired to. Neal claimed he was on board, but he also stayed away. I couldn't blame him. I know it was a blow to his male ego that added to the many blows I had dealt through the years.

His sudden distance only fueled me to take the homework seriously. It took a few personal sessions and another heated couple's session before I fully grasped that this could only be an answer to my prayer if I was serious about the process.

I wrote in my journal:

Neal desperately needs me to look at him with passion and longing in my eyes and to want him. We'll argue and he'll cry out, "If you can believe God will help you and do miracles in all things, then why can't you believe He can change you in this area?"

Good question. I know You can change my heart. So what keeps me from this?

What do I want?

I want to feel comfort and support from Neal. I want to be able to fall in love with him again so I can give rebirth to the sexual desire and intimacy. I want to finally have a relationship of total abandon—to feel like Neal is the only person to whom I can open myself up and give my all. I want the boys to see us in love and feel love from us. I want us to be a family that can sit and pray together, to come to each other with our worries, frustrations, and praises. To hold hands with each other and pray together.

I want Neal and me to be mighty partners, able to conquer any struggle in our family or lives because we have all we need and that's one another.

But we aren't on the same page. Maybe Neal is right. Maybe I am a hypocrite. He sees me now as a changed woman, leading teens and doing more at church than with my family, but yet I can't trust You, Lord, to heal me from this one aspect of my life.

CHAPTER 13

WAVES OF MERCY

Blessed be the God and Father of our Lord Jesus Christ, who in

his great mercy gave us a new birth to a living hope through the

resurrection of Jesus Christ from the dead. . . . In this you rejoice,

although now for a little while you may have to suffer through

various trials . . . so that the genuineness of your faith,

more precious than gold that is perishable even though

tested by fire, may prove to be for praise, glory,

and honor at the revelation of Jesus Christ.

1 Peter 1:3, 6–7

We worked diligently on the exercise that our therapist gave us. Within a few months, I slowly graduated a few levels, first holding his hand, then embracing the desire to be near him and touching without sexual intimacy, and then kissing. The wall became very thick and unyielding at this point. Physically, my body would react with personal performance anxiety, the need to please squeezing the air from my lungs.

I poured out my prayers to God in desperation for healing: *Lord, I pray for healing. I miss being with my husband as my husband. I know he is frustrated, and I want all of this to work out for both of us. I've cried out to You a dozen times for You to crack this wall that is between me and true intimacy. I need to break free! This is a continuous process for me, and I have faith that You will walk me through the wall and into healing. I want to be a woman who gladly accepts the gift of sexuality and gives this to her husband.*

Then one morning it dawned on me I had never followed through with the penance I'd been given before I became youth minister.

Afraid of how Neal would react but certain I needed to be clean and clear in our marriage, I convinced Neal to attend a one-day married couples' retreat. That afternoon, hand in hand, we went for a walk, still tentative and shy from the year of hard work we'd been through in counseling.

"I need to tell you something." A lump swelled in my throat.

"Okay."

"Remember that guy, Sean, I would talk to every now and then back when we lived in La Porte?"

He nodded. "Yeah, that guy you met in New Orleans?"

I swallowed and decided to blurt it out like ripping off a bandage fast so the sting would be quick. "Well, it was more than a friendship. I never saw him. He lived states away, but we became emotionally connected."

Neal stopped walking. The pain in his eyes stabbed into my heart.

"It was never physical."

"Like that makes a difference?"

I turned away, unable to look into his eyes any longer. "I'm so sorry. I haven't talked to him in over a year, since we moved. I don't even know why we were close. It was unfair to you and to our boys, and I am so sorry." The anticipation of the imminent anger that was to erupt made my fingers go numb.

The silence was excruciating as he processed it all.

Finally he grabbed my hands again. "I forgive you. I don't want to hear any more. I don't want to hear details. I don't want to know. It wasn't right and I don't like it, but we need to move on."

Just like that. He managed probably the three hardest words for a spouse to give and he did it with no other explanation: *I forgive you.*

Neal had his reasons for not wanting to know more or discuss it. I was happy to move on, but in hindsight, more should have been dealt with in the moment. Rushing or forcing forgiveness can often bring about resentment. Resentment does not fit well in marriage.

We held on to each other and let it be.

On equal ground, Neal and I felt the wall begin to crumble.

I wrote in my journal:

I don't believe I'll ever be "normal," as far as passion and desire go, but I do want to please my husband in a healthy way. I've been praying for this breakthrough for so long, and God has finally answered. Perseverance is key.

Last night, in my dreams, the greatest thing happened. I believe my subconscious healed itself. In the dream I was at a party at Paul's house (the friend who raped me when I was seventeen), and Matt was there (my boyfriend who died in the car accident), and in the dream I knew Matt was visiting from heaven. In the dream, we were all still at the age of seventeen, and I told Matt I wished he were alive so I could show him the love I had for him instead of pushing him away. Because he was there in front of me, I could. I was able to tell him I loved him. I felt alive and free!

Then in the dream Paul turned to me. "You wanted to be at my house. Don't deny that."

I was honest. "Yes, I did, and I'll admit that I might have eventually wanted to have sex with you, but not then and not like that. I said no."

The scene changed and I watched the rape take place, and the violence stunned me. I fought against him, but he kept trying, hurting me, pressing his fist into my mouth to keep me silent. It hit me like a splash of cold water on a blistering hot summer day: I did nothing wrong.

Through the dream, I finally accepted this obvious revelation. In a sense, I was awakened. God answered my prayer!

In a personal therapy session, I shared this revelation.

"I've always known deep down that it wasn't my *fault*," I said, "but I have always felt the shame and guilt from being at his house."

"Shannon, I know we've discussed those who've been your perpetrators of the two rapes, and you've forgiven them. We've talked about your older sister and how growing up in her shadow also affected your life. Did you send her the letter?"

I nodded. "She called. I can't even believe it."

Writing to Carrie added to the difficult steps I had to take to heal. Growing up in her shadow, I witnessed her in situations that a child should not witness. She held me as her only confidant, bringing me into her world of secrets, lies, and all the drugs that kept her emotionless.

When Carrie called, my heart sped up and my hands broke out into a sweat.

"Hey, I got your letter," she said.

"You did?" I waited for a barrage of curses and held my breath.

"Yeah. Shannon, I'm sorry. I didn't know I was hurting you. Most of the time I don't think I even realized you were around. All I wanted to do was escape."

It was the first time I'd heard her acknowledge anyone but herself.

To my therapist, I said, "It's not hard to forgive Carrie. I forgave her a long time ago."

Her actions were a product of the abuse inflicted by my grandfather. I felt sorrow for her more than I felt the need to forgive.

"But I wonder," my therapist said, pausing and tapping the notebook with her pen. "Have you forgiven yourself?"

My ego battled with the response. On one hand, I wanted to lash out and ask, "Why would I need to be forgiven?" and on the other, my spirit cried out in agony because I knew she'd hit the target.

I shrugged my shoulders in response because my throat was too tight to let out a peep.

"I want to do something with you that I've found to be successful when it comes to personal forgiveness," she said. "I don't advertise that I offer this service because it's been exploited in the media as a way to make up repressed memories. Some call it theophostic healing, but I don't go that deep into the memories. Through hypnosis, I would guide you through a meditation. Do you think you'd be interested?"

I'd been hypnotized before on a comedy stage for my cousin's bachelorette party. I knew I wouldn't be out of it and that I would be able to know what was going on but at the same time feel calm and secure.

"Sure," I said. I wanted to try anything.

I got comfortable on the couch.

"Okay, now I want you to focus on this object, and I'm going to count." She hung a medallion from a string and counted. "One, two, three, four, five . . . "

I don't know how far she counted before she told me to envision myself with Jesus beside me.

"Now imagine a place where you first felt like you were afraid or kept quiet. It might be a room or outside. Your mind will take you there."

It was a stream. The sound of water rushed and gurgled as it rose up and washed over river rocks. It wouldn't be until nine years later that the significance of this place would cause the most impact and healing in my life.

"Are you at the place?"

"Yes, it's a stream."

"Good. Now I want you to go to the girl inside of you that needs you most. The age you were when you first felt violated. She'll be standing there at the stream."

I was young. Very young.

With Jesus by my side, I knelt before the little girl and reached out to her. I held her in my arms. "I'm so sorry this happened to you," I told her. "I'm sorry you hurt and you're confused."

When I came to, my face was wet and my tears stained the pillow in my lap.

"How old was the little girl you went to?" she asked.

As clear as a high-definition movie, I recalled myself embracing the young girl. "Four, maybe five years old."

She jotted something on her notepad. "Why do you think you chose to see yourself so young and not as a teenager, when Paul raped you?"

The weight of a hand on my shoulder remained. Jesus's hand. The vision held me captive, and I wanted to cry again.

"I don't know. Maybe because that's when I started seeing my sister act out sexually?"

I looked at her as if maybe she had the answer.

"There could be a number of reasons why you chose to forgive yourself and reclaim your childhood. How do you feel?"

I sat up in on the couch. The warmth was gone from my shoulder, and my body felt lighter. "Good. Real good."

I thought I embraced forgiveness that day, but I failed to receive the gift of worth that forgiveness can offer. In a journal entry not long after this therapy session, I tried to put the confusion to words:

> *Lord, I am grateful to You for my life. There is so much You give me in a day—a smile or hug from my boys, Neal's love and acceptance, work done, rest, etc. Thank You for loving me. I know that You love me now, but there is still a child in me that struggles to think You thought much of me growing up. Lord, help me to be with You and to heal this inner child. All rationale says I should be able to overcome my idiosyncrasies. If I could heal myself, then I might be able to feel I am worthy. I know I deserve happiness, success, and pleasure. I haven't gotten to that point in my life where the fire within is let loose because I'm not able to accept what keeps me from receiving the joy. Lord, I know You will guide me. Please help me.*

There was something deeper that I couldn't touch, that I didn't *want* to touch, and in that moment I subconsciously (and on a level, consciously) chose to put it aside for a better time.

I couldn't focus on the little girl in me when I had my own little boy to think about. At the very moment, we were in the heart of counseling with Ryan. His pre-K4 teacher recommended we get him evaluated. The outbursts in class, tantrums, rocking, humming, and temper had escalated to such heights that it was no longer easy to brush them aside or put them off as my inability to parent.

Nine months Neal and I'd been in counseling, and nine months Neal had given up receiving love through the gift of intimacy. There was a hint of defeat because I knew I wasn't fully whole again. I wasn't "fixed," but I was on the mend and ready to embrace the new boundaries I'd learn to follow. Most importantly, I both *wanted* and *needed* Neal.

Healed "enough," I said goodbye to my therapist and proclaimed Neal and I had graduated from therapy. I could be intimate *enough*. It was all I could do for myself because my son needed me more.

CHAPTER 14

MESSENGERS

And for this reason we too give thanks to God unceasingly, that,

in receiving the word of God from hearing us,

you received not a human word but, as it truly is,

the word of God, which is now at work in you who believe.

1 Thessalonians 2:13

Two months of twice-a-week evaluations involving play therapy, tests, one-on-one therapy, and other extensive evaluating measures led us to hear this conclusion for Ryan: "Your son is very intelligent for his age—genius level, with an IQ of 142. He has impulsivity issues and ADHD."

I looked over at Ryan, who threw his little body into the chair on wheels so that it slammed him into the wall. The impact made him fall out of the chair. He laughed, got up, and did it again. Over and over.

"It is my recommendation that he be put on medication to help focus the ADHD and impulsivity, and also come in for play therapy once a week."

Neal clenched the arm o his seat and dug his nails into the fabric. "I don't want my son on medication."

The doctor looked at Ryan as his chair hit the wall and then looked back at us. "Mr. Deitz, I understand putting your child on medication is scary, but let me put it to you this way. Your son has the capability to be a major asset to society"—she took a dramatic pause—"or a detriment. It is unlikely there will be an in between, especially if he isn't given something to help him to slow down and communicate on his level as well as focus his behaviors."

Neal and I looked at each other. I could tell he was thinking about his family as I was thinking about mine. Neither of our parents wanted us to put him on medication.

"He's fine. He's just a boy. Don't turn him into a zombie," Neal said.

We needed to do what we could to give Ryan the opportunity to be an asset.

We took her recommendation to our pediatrician. The first sixty seconds of the appointment, Ryan jumped on and off the table at least six times. Dr. Gallo watched him do this with fascination and a telling smile. He reached out and tousled Ryan's thick hair. "A little hyperactive, are we?"

He confirmed the psych evaluation but was against the play therapy. "This kid is so smart, the last thing you want to do is make him feel like he has done something wrong. Sending him to play therapy might cause him to set himself apart as different than everyone else, and we don't want that. Mark my words, he'll be off this medication and an upstanding young man, smarter than you and me, before you know it."

Trust. That's what we needed to do. Trust in God's plan and the recommendations of the qualified.

Within the first few weeks of Ryan taking the medication, I was on my knees singing the Lord's praise because it was a godsend. It didn't make him a zombie or less of a little boy. It helped him slow down enough to interact with others instead of overreacting to their desire to play or be near him.

With Ryan's diagnosis and our couple's therapy behind us, we settled into a new norm of life in Kingwood.

Our sexual intimacy issues were better—not perfect or what either of us would consider normal, but better. I no longer felt the anxiety or frustration that would tighten my chest during intimate moments. I had healthy boundaries and no longer forced myself to be intimate when I didn't want to be.

That was behind us. We were in love again, and though we were still on uneven ground when it came to our faith life, we at least were on the same road.

That summer, I made a pilgrimage to Italy and Germany with the youth group, attending the World Youth Day festivities in Cologne, Germany, and my life took a turn.

I've had strange things happen in my life. I've seen evil in its purest form. I've seen angels and I've felt God's presence in such a way that I felt as if I could kiss His cheek. And yet, this experience—this was one that I knew many wouldn't understand. I received a "message" from someone who called me out by name. He found me in a field of 1.2 million people and insisted he had a message specifically for me.

August 20, 2005

Good morning, Lord. I experienced my most troubled night ever, but amidst the strangeness it was also spiritual and fully of You. You protected me, and You spoke to me. I need to write this down to make sense of it. A huge part of me feels as if all this is drama created out of my mind, my imagination, yet I have witnesses to prove it happened. Then I feel crazy, yet remarkably it all makes sense, and it is as if a puzzle piece has been snapped into place.

First, that man, Brian, whom I met on the bridge in Germany to see Pope Benedict XVI seemed to be an answer from You for moving forward in my writing, because when we were introduced, that is what we discussed: our mutual desire to write a Catholic Bible study. When we met, we exchanged e-mails and then went our separate ways with the understanding we'd e-mail as soon as my first novel was complete.

Three days later, at midnight in the field, I was woken up by my name being called. One of the women in the group pointed at me, and the next thing I knew, Brian was standing over my sleeping bag.

"Come with me," he said. "I have something I need to tell you."

I can't explain what came over me in that very moment. It was like a rush of certainty. I knew I needed to go with him. At the same time, I kept thinking, How did he find me? *Because we weren't even in the spot we were assigned to, and we were at least eighty thousand people away from where we were originally assigned.*

As I struggled to get my shoes on, one of the teens in my group said, "Bring her back in one hour!"

I smiled.

We walked at a fast pace, and I tried to gather my bearings.

"How did you find me?" I asked.

"Honestly, I don't know. I was led to the spot, and then I started calling out your name."

He walked me to the edge of the hill where the pope was to say Mass the next morning. It was covered with votive candles, and I stood there mesmerized by the flickering flames. I felt a chest-tightening sadness come over me for everyone attending the extraordinary event who didn't get it.

I turned away and looked at Brian. He had an intense look on his face as he stared at me. I walked over to the chairs set out for the morning Mass and sat down. He followed and did the same.

"What is it you obviously want to say?" I asked.

I wasn't scared, Lord, but I had an odd feeling in my stomach.

He looked at me then with these big piercing eyes. "Do you see good or evil in me?"

My skin prickled at the familiarity of this scenario. I'd stared through the eyes of evil when I was eight years old; I didn't want to live through that again. The difference was that I didn't see evil. I felt good from him, which made me confused. I had no fear.

"I see good in you," I said.

His look was intense, as if his life depended on our conversation.

"I need to apologize for bringing you over here," he said, "but I need to let you know there is something that draws me to you, and not just me, but I know you draw many to you. You're like the candles out there, except the light of them bundled together that can never be snuffed out."

What was I to say? I listened.

"I truly believe God led me to Germany to meet you. I don't like to travel or fly, and I never wanted to come on this trip. Then I met you and it was clear to me, and I haven't been able to sleep since."

Unnerved by this claim, I felt the familiar sense that maybe he was drawn to me for the wrong reasons. So I took a second.

"Please don't think of me as arrogant," I said, "but for whatever reason this seems to happen to me. It is my weakness the devil preys upon, my need to feel wanted by men and something they long for. But I've gotten caught in this trap before. I don't doubt God brought us together for a good, holy cause, but the devil finds that niche to seep in and corrupt God's pure motives. I've given in, thankfully not completely, to Satan's tricks, but I am strong enough now to stop it before it begins."

He nodded. "I don't have the strength, but I knew you did, which is why I needed to tell you not to contact me. You can't e-mail me. I cannot see you or speak to you again."

I was stunned by this and how adamant he was. His urgency shook me deep.

"You know, even in this greatest spiritual place there is much evil. You are in danger," he said.

Evil was present. He shook uncontrollably. He took my hand, and I felt eerily calm and knew I needed to listen.

"This is the strangest thing, and I don't mean to scare you, but I just know—I can't explain it—but I know there is something about you that attracts both good and evil," he said.

"What do you see? Why would someone want to hurt me?"

He let go of my hand and grabbed me by the shoulders. "Shannon, what you have to say is important. You will help many people, and this will not please everyone, because you have something new to say."

I thought about this, how it solidified some thoughts I had but never knew if they were of You or my overactive imagination. For some reason, I thought about my moment of surrender to You on my bedroom floor.

"Are you afraid to die?" I asked.

He didn't hesitate. "Yes. I like my life too much. Are you?"

I shook my head no.

He appeared troubled. "I wish I could have that certainty."

I knew I needed to tell him what You gave me that changed me. "You haven't fully received the Holy Spirit," I said. "When you have the Spirit alive within you, then you have certainty and peace of knowing all is good. Even when you tell me these things, I am not surprised and I am not scared. I wish you were stronger, because I know the Bible study we could have done together would have been good."

He studied me for a long time. "I know for sure I needed to tell you and to warn you."

"Do you feel like you are crazy because you are saying these things? I mean, I don't think you're crazy. I'm just wondering how new this is to you?"

"Yes, I don't even feel like myself."

I got up. "I need to get back to the group." I didn't want to be there with him anymore.

We combed our way through the thousands and thousands of people, and he spoke really fast about what he felt I needed to do. He said my writings would help a lot of people.

I looked at him in disbelief. "You don't even know my story. How can you know what I write will help others?"

He shrugged his shoulders. "I told you, I just know."

We walked in silence for a bit until I got the nerve to ask him what I'd been wanting to ask since we sat down. "Brian, I don't want you to get mad or offended, but was there ever even a slight hint of a moment where you were going to, or had set out to, hurt me?"

He looked at me with such a look of bewilderment, I was embarrassed I asked.

"How did you know?" he asked. "I mean, it was a brief moment and I am ashamed it even came over me, but I know that's why I can't be near your or talk to you. I can't and don't want to harm you."

Deep inside, I knew this was true all along. I knew You orchestrated a battle of good and evil before my eyes, not masked in colors.

We stopped in front of my section of the field. I felt compelled to give him my own message.

"Brian, you are good, and I forgive you," I said.

His face rose with hope. "Do you believe in karma — those that do bad get back what's coming to them?"

"I believe everyone deserves a chance to be forgiven and it's God who will decide if they get their comebacks."

He reached out and grabbed me by the wrists. "Write, Shannon. Every night, write on that book now. I don't know what all happened to you, but I wish I could've known you then to protect you. But maybe God needed whatever you've gone through to happen."

Bewildered, I gave him a hug. "Okay, then this is good-bye."

One of the teens from my group stood in our section, looking for me. When he saw me, he came and gave me a hug, and I started to cry. It was too much to take in. Too surreal, Lord. But I know, impending danger or not, he was a messenger for me. It is clarification that whether it's scary or not, I know I have You, and even though my path seems surreal, what You've chosen for me is real and I trust in You.

When we returned to the States, I didn't know how to embrace my life as a mother of two young boys, driving a beat-up old Suburban and going to YMCA soccer games. The role of youth minister I could manage because it gave me the ability to be entrenched in faith and religion at all times, which is what I held on to after receiving that crazy message.

But I couldn't tell Neal. He was my best friend, and yet I couldn't tell him. I was afraid if he knew I took a walk with a strange man and then this strange man told me all of these crazy things, he would think I was insane and lock me up. I knew what it looked like to someone who wasn't there.

I knew it was far-fetched for the "real world," and even though Neal knew about all of the other spiritual happenings in my life, he was quick to dismiss them. He never made fun of me, nor did he ever tell me he didn't believe me, but it was a story I'd tell that didn't need further discussion. This particular story involved a real, live man and not some ethereal demonic spirit or angel.

After a week, I couldn't take it anymore. I e-mailed Brian:

August 27, 2005
Hi,

    I realize you said you simply needed to have no contact. So consider this the one and only time I'll send you an e-mail. I've been considering this contact all week, and as much as a huge part of me is against it and very willing to give you your wishes to not see or hear from me, the other part really needs to know it was all real.

Who knows, maybe you don't even remember me or the conversation we had. I have questions that I know I'll never have answered. I don't want to get into a back-and-forth trying to have that accomplished. So I won't ask.

I haven't been able to write since I've been back. Not that I don't want to. So many things are keeping me from it, which makes me flash to your earnest plea and I want to scream. Anyway.

Well, take care, God bless, and if you will, send me a short note so I know it was real.

Shannon Deitz

He wrote back:

August 28, 2005
Hello Shannon,

Bless you for your message. I am fine, and, yes, I recall every detail of our conversation, that night at Merrien Field in front of the candle-covered hill. What I said to you wasn't fluff, and it wasn't said lightly. I'll never forget.

I've received reconciliation for my sinful thoughts toward you, and I try to dismiss further thoughts, but it is difficult. Please don't contact me again.

You have to keep writing. You are an angel sent to a greater, specific purpose. You have to know that. And damn anyone who stands in your way. Were I stronger, I would follow you to the ends of this life.

I pray for you every single day.

B

There it was: validation that I didn't dream up the entire evening. Yet it was still crazy.

Who says these things? I'm an angel and "I'd follow you to the ends of this life"? I couldn't take it anymore.

The e-mail was sent on a Sunday evening. I printed it out and put it in my journal.

Monday morning, I took the kids to school and went to morning Mass. Through the homily, the priest spoke about a friend of his who was given a specific purpose in life but the enemy was determined to thwart his efforts. I could not stop the tears from falling as I listened to a story that paralleled the crazy life I lived.

I'm not special, I thought. *This is crazy. I'm insane and egotistical, thinking this has anything to do with me.*

At the end of Mass, I went up to the priest, whom I'd come to know well in the year and a half I'd been working for him.

"Hello, Ms. Shannon." He leaned down and brought me into a bear hug.

"Fr. B, do you have time to talk?" My voice cracked, and tears threatened to force me into a bumbling idiot. "I really need some advice."

"Well, I think I can spare a minute. I'm headed out of town, but you can walk with me to my office." He finished taking off his vestments and locked the sacristy door.

I was too embarrassed to begin on the short walk to his office. Instead, I caught him up on happenings with the youth department.

Safely inside the confines of the four walls, I sat down in the worn leather chair and felt my throat constrict with the onset of tears.

"I don't know where to begin. I don't want to make you late."

He handed me a tissue. "I'll be fine. Just start from the beginning."

For the first time since it began when I was a little girl, I told my entire spiritual story, from the near abduction to be a cult sacrifice to seeing the enemy at my aunt's home to witnessing angels and demons battle it out in my bedroom, all the way up to the encounter with Brian and his message.

"Am I crazy?" I asked. "Because if I am, please tell me and I'll be glad to go commit myself."

I almost *wanted* to be told I was crazy so it would make sense.

The priest laughed and smiled so that his eyes twinkled. "You're not crazy, Shannon. This is a gift. Events like this happen all the time, but most of us aren't aware. It is the spiritual gift of discernment. We all have spiritual gifts, and we are stronger in some than others. This is your strong spiritual gift."

He believes me. I wept with relief.

He reached out and patted my hand.

His time was short, so the conversation was quick, and I gave him a hug and thanked him. All I needed was someone who, in my opinion, would have the highest spiritual authority other than God to validate me.

A weight lifted, and I could breathe and function again.

The following evening, I had a late-night adoration hour, which is an hour of prayer before the Blessed Sacrament. During this time I would usually journal, meditate, and sometimes rest in prayer. That night I'd taken my prayer journal to document what the priest had said and how I felt encouraged to continue writing the book and tell others about my story.

It was 1 a.m. when I got home. Exhausted, I went straight to bed.

At 6 a.m., I was woken up by Neal, who was on his way out to work. He'd already been out to his truck and found a shredded piece of paper on the ground. It was the e-mail correspondence between Brian and me. It must have fallen out of the journal and landed on the ground, where the dog got ahold of it and tore it apart.

"What's this?" Neal clenched the paper in his hand.

Still groggy from sleep, I squinted my eyes to adjust to the darkness within the room and the light that came from behind him in the doorway. "What?"

"It looks like some e-mail between you and a guy? It says something about following you to the ends of this life? Who is this guy?" His voice dripped with a mixture of hurt and anger.

I froze. *How do I tell him the entire truth in a matter of a second so he understands it's not what he thinks it is?*

"It's hard to explain," I said.

"What do you mean it's hard to explain? You met some guy while you were in Germany on a pilgrimage?"

"No, no, it wasn't like that. It's not what you think it is *at all.*"

I silently prayed he'd come sit next to me on the bed so I could tell him everything.

"Whatever." He stomped out of the house.

I lay back down and could hear the blood pumping in my ears. *God, what do I do? What do I say?*

I couldn't let him get to work and think I'd betrayed him again. I called his cell phone and cried when he answered. The entire story rushed out, like letting the air out of a balloon.

He remained quiet until I was done.

"So there was nothing else between you two?" he said. "How did he find you? Why did you go with a stranger?"

It felt awful. Stating the truth only brought on more questions. "I don't know. I can't explain it."

By the grace of God, he either believed me enough to let it go or he thought it so outlandish I must have made up the entire story. Either way, he brushed it off as he had done with the other spiritual events in my life as "Shannon's imagination."

I didn't mind. I knew I had proof, and the e-mail was the best proof. I printed it out again and replaced it in my journal.

CHAPTER 15

SMALL MIRACLE

And the prayer of faith will save the sick person,

and the Lord will raise him up.

If he has committed any sins, he will be forgiven.

James 5:15

A woman on a mission, I wrote as if my life depended upon the completion of the book. During this time, I talked more openly to the teens about some of my experiences, including the spiritual warfare. It was interesting to have them reveal their own stories and find a sense of relief that I would share mine.

During a diocesan youth minister's retreat, I shared openly with my small group, and for the first time I had adults listen. I could see they didn't think I was crazy, and they didn't judge me. Instead, they all encouraged me to keep talking about my story. A few invited me out to their youth groups to share what I'd been through.

Then the big break came, and I was asked to speak at an ecumenical event in front of eight hundred middle school and high school teenagers. I couldn't help but think about Brian and his message: *Tell your story*.

Am I bold enough? The thought of getting up in front of twenty-five—let alone eight hundred—made my knees weak and stomach churn. There was no way I could manage to do this.

In the midst of writing about the deepest spiritual attack within my college years and faced with the fear of speaking in public, I heard the lies: *You are not good enough. Don't do it; they'll be bored. No one really believes you.*

God, help me. I was tired of the battle. I went to Barnes and Noble and searched and searched for a book or something to help validate the occurrences I'd been through with spiritual warfare.

I tapped my fingers impatiently on the spines of a row of books.

"That's a good book." A gentleman in a suit pointed to one of the books I tapped.

"Yes, I've read it, as well," I said. "It's good, but I'm looking for a book on spiritual warfare."

"Really? I know *exactly* who you need to see. Dr. Pat Carter. He's an expert on the subject." The man pulled a business card from his wallet and a pen from his breast pocket. "Here is his number." He scribbled a number on the back of the card.

Stunned, I took the card. "Funny. I was just asking God to help."

"Well, I guess that makes me your divine appointment, then."

I nodded in agreement and left the bookstore.

It took me a few minutes before I realized what had taken place. God had placed him in my path.

I called the number, and Dr. Pat picked up on the second ring.

"I was given your number by Mr.—"I flipped the card over to get the name—"Mr. Heines. He said you know some things on spiritual warfare?"

"Ah, yes. Yes, of course. I've been teaching on the subject for over thirty years. Why don't we meet to talk about it?"

That is when I found out he lived at the edge of my street. I asked God for help, and He gave me someone within walking distance.

A spirit of goodness and joy permeated through Dr. Pat. His eyes lit up when he opened the door.

"Hello, Shannon. Come in. Come in," he said.

He moved with ease. Besides his thick white hair, there was nothing about him to give testament to his age.

Framed pictures of men and women closer to my parents' age filled the room, along with pictures of teenagers, toddlers, and babies. In one, the entire family was together—from the looks of it, close to thirty people. He was old enough to be my grandfather. Tension and nervousness that had built up in my shoulders calmed down, and I relaxed.

"You are a young woman," he said. "What brings you to wanting to know more about spiritual warfare?"

What do I say? I see spirits? I see demons? I feel evil? Strange people give me messages and at the same time fight back an urge to hurt me?

I froze.

He smiled, and his mustache curled into his nose. "Do you experience things that you can't explain?"

He gets it.

I swallowed. "Yes. It's really hard to talk about because I've not told any one everything that I've seen. I feel like I'm crazy sometimes."

"Oh, you're not crazy." He leaned back in his chair. "I lived in Mexico for thirty years and helped counsel many people who've seen demons." He explained a few stories of others who had experiences similar to what I had.

"I know exactly what you're talking about," I said.

He gets it. He gets me.

I allowed everything to spill forth like a dam that burst. It felt good to tell it again. I'd told Fr. B most of it, but this time I didn't hold anything back.

Dr. Pat scooted his chair up close to mine so that our knees touched. He took my hands in his and looked me in the eyes. "You are not crazy. The enemy nips at your heels because he doesn't want you to bring others closer to God. This is a battle you'll fight for the rest of your life on earth. Let's pray together."

We met at least once or twice a month to pray together or to talk about the progress of my book. We became friends and he talked to me about his projects, and I would in turn pray over him.

Between meeting with Dr. Pat on spiritual warfare and meeting with my spiritual advisor, a Monsignor priest who was retired and living at the seminary in Houston, I had plenty of spiritual guidance and encouragement to be bold in the statement God had given me through my life.

Being bold in my marriage remained a struggle. I searched for every opportunity to give Neal and me a chance to grow spiritually together. When Neal agreed to attend a *Theology of the Body* seminar put on by Christopher West, I was shocked.

"Whatever," he said. "I'll go."

I knew he did it to appease me, and possibly to shut me up, and that was fine.

Theology of the Body is a series of encyclicals (talks) given by Pope John Paul II to a young adult audience. The focus was on the gift of our spirituality, the gift of sex, and God's intention for us as man and woman.

Neal and I heard the same talks in the same seminar, but we left with different takeaways.

I appreciated Christopher discussing the importance of the man respecting a woman's body and the sacredness of what God created, that a woman should not be demeaned by pornography, strip joints, and the like. He had discussed the gift of intercourse between a husband and wife. I longed for what he described, but deep inside I felt a pang of shame and guilt. There was something I couldn't give voice to that kept me from receiving such a gift.

Neal, on the other hand, left halfway through the full-day seminar. He mumbled something about his stomach giving him issues and, knowing we knew others there, that someone would give him a ride home. So he left.

When I got home, I found a note:

Shannon:

First, I would like to say I'm sorry for all you might have gone through, and I'm sorry if I was not there in the capacity you needed me to be. After listening to Christopher West, I could not have felt any more ashamed of my behavior and attitude about what you might have gone through in the past.

I was very selfish if I ever did anything but lend support or help you with your problems in any way other than complaining. A lot of what I heard and learned hit a certain spot in my heart. I know I am a good person, but there is so much more I can be and do for us and our family. I do want that kind of relationship with you and would love more than anything for you to be happy and comfortable with me in a marital way.

I know it's not easy for you, but I will do what I can to make you comfortable. I have been blessed in so many ways, yet I feel horrible about a lot of things, and I will do anything to get us on the same page with our lives. I am not a sex fiend by any stretch of the imagination, but I can accept I view certain things certain ways and hopefully, with your help, I can grow from this and strengthen our relationship.

I do love you very much, and I truly want the best for us. I will admit I sometimes feel taken advantage of, but I can also attribute that to selfish reasons, and I am doing my best to overcome all of my shortcomings. You will need to bear with me because there are a lot of them and it will take time. I love you and hope you enjoyed the seminar and got from it what you needed. It was a lot for me to take in.

Please don't hesitate to be open with me and let me in on what's going on in your mind. I might not agree with you 100 percent of the time, but I do love you and I will do my best to help out.

Love,

Neal

Neal never ceased to amaze me. When I felt he had every right to walk out the door, he showed his vulnerability. This note gave me a sense of strength and courage in knowing we were doing something right.

I felt encouraged and ready for God to speak through me to eight hundred teenagers. But six weeks before the event was to take place, I ran into a medical issue I could no longer ignore. Cursed with heavy and painful menstrual cycles from the moment I hit puberty, they were now debilitating. Often I would come home an hour or two before picking up the boys from school because I couldn't keep my eyes open. The loss of blood left me anemic and void of energy. It was a miracle I worked with teens because my energy levels were at an extreme low. The teens helped keep me going.

In a vulnerable position, with my feet in stirrups, I was given the news.

"You're hemorrhaging. You need a hysterectomy," Dr. Gunther, my new gynecologist, informed me. "Even if you were to get pregnant, your uterus would not be able to hold the pregnancy."

Even if. She didn't know that for the past two years I secretly hoped Neal's vasectomy was unsuccessful. My periods were so erratic, I would bleed for months and then not bleed at all, which led me to purchase pregnancy tests and then be faced with the obvious fact that I had made the decision to never see a plus sign again.

But I didn't know I would come to a place of letting go of the rage that held me prisoner. And I didn't know I would be led to a place of understanding as the truth of the Catholic Church's teaching became clearer. It was slow at first, but in time I embraced the religion that nurtured my faith. Three years before, I didn't know I'd be led to a job within the Catholic Church, to have a priest as a boss, and to feel compelled to confess I asked Neal to do the vasectomy. I couldn't blame Neal for refusing a reversal because of the pain he'd endured the first time around.

I did not foresee the devastating ache I'd have inside when I saw a little girl hold on to her daddy's hand and realized I kept Neal from knowing that kind of love, or how incomplete my family would feel.

Like it was a quick and an insignificant procedure. I sat up, worried Dr. Gunther would go right in and yank it out. I was thirty-one years old. It *was* significant. There would be no going back on past mistakes and making things right. It meant my family would be complete as is. I had no options.

I was given two weeks to get prepared, prepped, and in surgery for a permanent life change.

I sat in my car after the appointment. The white painted lines of the parking spaces came together as my vision blurred. I thought about the youth ministry job God led me into only a year after making the decision to have the vasectomy and the dozens of times I heard "When are you going to have another baby?" and shrugged in answer, swallowing back the hypocrisy. Now I wouldn't have to lie to the teens.

Another deep pain cut through my chest.

I prayed, *You called me into that job. I told You I was the last person You wanted because of all I've been through and done.*

For one brief second, I allowed the obvious thought to escape: *This is what I deserve.*

God answered in my heart: *I bring good from everything. You are a nurturer to the teens and to your children. Trust in My plan.*

The timing, despite the devastating situation, was impeccable. I would have the surgery, stay one night in the hospital, and then recoup at home for six weeks—which was one week before the keynote.

The surgery went without complications. I was allergic to anesthesia medicine, which made me nauseated. I threw up for the first few hours after coming out of the fog.

Neal brought me home, and I did as instructed: I lay on the couch and didn't move. Friends from church brought over meals, and the teens had pitched in to get me an iPod, which was the newest gadget at the time. I never felt more loved and taken care of than I did in those first few days of recovery. It took my mind off the void within me. The teens kept me from curling up in a ball in my room, exhausted and in tears. A baby would never grow inside of me again.

Despite the decision for Neal to undergo a vasectomy four years before, I had held out hope for the last two years a miracle would occur and God would reverse my decision. At the time, it felt like the right decision. Mentally, I couldn't fathom a child. But that was then. Neal and I were two different people then. We'd matured, suffered through a major drought in our marriage, and had finally landed in a good, compatible place. Plus, I was calmer now, no longer flying off the handle as much as I used to, the hostility waned. I no longer feared I would harm my children in any way.

But it wasn't to be.

I knew within my spirit this was a blessing. God said, *Don't let this be of a concern to you. You have your family and your church family. Trust Me in your path.*

Five days post-surgery, I ended up back in the hospital. We'd eaten a scrumptious Italian meal of sausage and peppers brought by one of the families of the teens I ministered to. Neal sat at my feet as I lay recovering on the couch and the kids were tucked in bed.

My stomach gurgled and my palms got pasty.

"I don't feel too good." I sat up.

"What do you need?" Neal got off the couch and stood in front of me.

"I feel dizzy." The floor loomed in my vision and then faded away.

"Let me get you some TUMS, and you go to bed." He pulled me off the couch and directed me to our bedroom.

I stumbled my way into the room and lay down. Beads of sweat fell off my chin, and I felt the drops hit my chest.

Neal walked into the room with a bottle of water and the TUMS. "You aren't looking too great," he said. "You sure you're okay?"

I swallowed back the urge to vomit. "Maybe it was the sausage."

I took the TUMS with the rest of my medications and tried to get some sleep. A case of shivers coursed through my body, and this time I couldn't swallow the need to vomit. I didn't make it to the bathroom.

Neal heard the commotion from the living room.

When he saw me, he gagged. He left the room and came back with a thermometer.

I'd managed to crawl to the toilet.

"Let's take your temperature," he said.

It was 103.

"You need to go to the hospital."

"How? Who'll watch the boys? We don't need to get them up."

"Shannon, you can't wait till morning. Call Christina. I'll get your cell."

Christina was the assistant youth minister and didn't have children. It was late in the night, and she answered on the first ring.

"Hey, sorry to call you so late," I said, then gagged and held the phone away. The contents in my stomach wouldn't stay down.

"Shannon? Shannon? Hello?"

Neal came in with a wet washcloth and wiped my mouth.

"Could you take me to the hospital?" I said. "Something's going on, and we don't want to get the boys out of bed."

"Oh my gosh. Yes, of course. I'm on my way."

It took thirty minutes on a normal day to get downtown to the Women's Hospital of Texas. We got there in fifteen. I held on to a trash bag and apologized every time I had to use it.

"It's okay," Christina said. "You don't look so good."

"I feel as bad as I look, then."

A week later, I wrote about the ordeal in my journal:

Tuesday, March 7, 2006

> *This morning's reading from the devotional my mom gave me in the hospital says, "Today let the direction of your life be guided by God's hand."*
>
> *I smile because I believed it before, but I LIVE it now. And when I mean before, I mean just last week.*
>
> *So much has gone on in this past week, writing it down is my testament to God. When I went in for the hysterectomy, all was good. I came home, everything*

was healing well, and there were no problems except for a bit of cabin fever.

Then Monday rolled around, and that evening I was restless. I knew something was wrong. At about 1 a.m., the nausea kicked in, and by 3 a.m. I was vomiting profusely. At 4 a.m. Chris (the assistant youth minister) came to get me and take me back to the hospital. After suffering the long ride, I made it to the treatment center, convulsing, shaking, and begging them to knock me out.

After three tries with an IV, a line was finally inserted and the nausea brought to a calm—not gone, but calm. Then X-rays, ultrasounds, and my doctor checking me internally. Everything was fine.

Perplexed, the doctors had no idea what was wrong. There was no fever, and the white blood count was normal.

By Wednesday (Tuesday I was delirious and don't recall the entire day), I was discharged. By the time I got home, I felt odd again. That night I ran a fever, and on Thursday had an extreme case of diarrhea and my temperature kept rising above 101. It took all afternoon before I relented. I needed to call the doctor. She ordered me back to the hospital, and I was admitted once again.

This time I had a high white blood cell count of 22,000, when the normal count is 10,000, which meant there was an infection somewhere inside. My fever wouldn't drop below 101, and my side hurt.

Friday morning I was sent in for a CT scan. That was not fun. Drinking the barium was like drinking liq-

uid hell. *Having then to go for the scan, have an enema inserted into my rectum, and hold it for thirty minutes was a chore, to say the least. Yet I kept a smile on my face. Peace. I felt a calming peace that kept me certain I would be fine. The nurses and doctors did their job, so I felt like there was no need to complain.*

Once I was back in my room, I finally heard the results: appendicitis.

What?! I laughed aloud. God had a sense of humor. So, really, what was I to do or say? Nothing could change it. I wasn't dying. I had to live with the fact I was going to be cut into and go through another recovery, but many more people suffered worse news.

Everyone was called to pray. My mom rushed down from Dallas to be by my side, God bless her. At 8 p.m. I realized I was not having surgery until the next morning. At 10:30 p.m. the surgeon came in and explained what the CT scan really showed. It was not appendicitis. I had an infection that had formed a pocket over my appendix and a part of my bowel. At the moment it was contained, but that explained why the megadoses of antibiotics were not bringing my white blood cell count down. He said it would be a delicate procedure to remove the infection. He would have to cut me open and extract the infection, the appendix, and possibly a part of my bowel. If that was the case, I could end up with a colostomy bag. I would have staples, a drainage tube—the whole nine yards.

Not fun.

But my way of handling uncomfortable moments and news was through humor. So I asked the doctor if he could give me a tummy tuck while he was in there. He was shocked I could kid him. "What can I say? I'm not dying," I said.

Surgery was scheduled for 7 a.m. At 3:30 a.m., a nurse came in to take some blood. At 6 a.m., my surgeon came in and explained they were taking me for more X-rays. Back in my room at 7 a.m., I wondered why I wasn't being prepped for surgery. Then all three doctors entered who had worked with me: my ob-gyn, the surgeon, and the infectious disease doctor.

They stood at the foot of my bed. One of the surgeons spoke up. "You are something else."

I smiled. "What do you mean?"

"Overnight, your white blood cell count went from 22,000 to 10,000. This sudden drop does not usually happen. Which is why we took more X-rays. They show the infection has diminished from the bowel and appendix. We don't need to operate."

Praise be to God!

Ah, I can't help but cry, thinking about the glory of God in heaven and all the people who prayed for me. Their prayers were answered! I am still humbled to think so many prayed, and I wanted them to know God listened to them.

I stayed in the hospital until Sunday night on IV antibiotics. Here I am at home, a little weak, a little tired, but doing great because I didn't have surgery!

They said the infection is still there but going away, and I still have to heal from the hysterectomy, but now I can make it for the keynote.

God taught me a lot this past week. I realize how I don't want to get any praise—truly. I've felt it before, but I know it now. All of those parishioners, friends, co-workers, and all the teens—they all had faith and prayed for me. I want them to have a heavenly host come upon them and raise them up. And God—oh, what work He did to answer them, all of His angels fighting the demons that tried so hard to knock me down. Praise God!

It's not a wonder that I got home on Sunday night and suffered through a terrible attack of the enemy. I was weak, but my weakness is still covered by the blood of the Lamb, Jesus Christ.

I prayed.

Christ prevailed.

My prayer partner, Dr. Pat, came over Monday morning and we prayed together to dispel the enemy. I am at peace. This last week was a fight, a battle, on many levels, but God took the chance to show His truth.

Thank you, thank you, thank you, Lord. Holy, holy, holy is Your name.

A little weak and still healing, I managed to deliver the keynote, "God's Plan for Your Life," to the eight hundred middle school and high school students. Unbeknownst to me, a man in the audience videotaped the keynote, which landed in the hands of the folks at Franciscan University in Steubenville, Ohio, who put on the massive Catholic Youth Conferences. By September, I got an invitation to serve on their speaking team.

I didn't seek this path. God planned it.

CHAPTER 16

RUNNING THE RACE

For I am already being poured out like a libation,

and the time of my departure is at hand. I have competed well;

I have finished the race; I have kept the faith.

2 Timothy 4:6–7

God gave me a small miracle and blessed me with gifts and talents I never knew to ask for and never felt worthy of desiring or receiving. Yet the closer I got to God, the more I became aware of the behaviors, attitudes, and bad habits that did not please God. I was acutely aware of my selfishness as a mother, a wife, a friend—even as a daughter and granddaughter.

The older the kids got, the more demanding they were of my time. The time I spent playing board games or doing something the boys wanted to do was determined by whether or not it fit within my time frame or if I was in the mood.

Within my marriage, I took advantage of our rejuvenated love and Neal's acceptance of what I'd been through by doing more of what pleased me, which was ministry. If I was asked to speak or to lead a retreat, I went, regardless of the fact Neal was left home with the kids or that it took away from our time together. I reasoned that God called me to it and I enjoyed it, so I did it. Friendships had gone to the wayside, and the times we took to visit my family became scarce.

Fleeting moments of uncertainty and guilt shone through, but I didn't know how to balance what I knew was His calling along with my main vocation as wife and mother.

In the midst of the springtime ministry activities, senior send-off, and graduation banquet, I received a phone call from my mother. Sweetgraw, my ninety-five-year-old grandmother, was ill. If I wanted some time with her, I needed to make it happen.

Neal didn't hesitate to encourage me to take off for a few days and make the five-hour drive to spend some one-on-one time with Sweetgraw.

"Sweetgraw, I'm coming in Tuesday to see you," I said when I called her. "I'm going to spend the entire day with you. Is that okay?"

"Oh my, yes. I'm going to mark it on my calendar, and no one else is going to intrude. Oh, Shannon, I'm so excited to see you."

She wanted her time with me, and that made me feel special.

Sweetgraw lived in an assisted-living retirement community. She had her own apartment, but meals were served in a common cafeteria, which she loved the most because she would flaunt her visitor at lunch like we were her latest accessory. "Grenadine have you met my granddaughter, Shannon? She came all the way from Houston to see me." From table to table, she held my hand as she steered her scooter with the other to get every unfortunate soul's attention who didn't have a visitor.

By the sixth person I met, I politely squeezed Sweetgraw's hand. "Why don't we get our table, Sweetgraw. Let's let people eat their lunch."

I was amused with her insistence to parade me around, but it wasn't just me. She had visitors every day, and it was the same for them. It might have been her own selfish behavior—to show the world how loved she was—but it also made me proud to make her feel loved.

We spent the day talking, playing Spite 'n' Malice, one of her favorite card games, and saying the rosary with Mother Angelica on EWTN. When we ended the rosary, she got very quiet and I could see she was crying.

"Sweetgraw, what's wrong?" I reached over and squeezed her hand.

She looked at me—I mean, *really* looked at me, where her eyes penetrated my soul. "I am so tired."

"Well, Sweetgraw, you can lie down and take a nap." Her sudden seriousness troubled me.

"No, Shannon, I'm tired of not being well." Her grip tightened on my hand. The bones of her fingers left indents in my skin.

I got it. She was ninety-five, her body riddled with a cancer they couldn't do anything about because she was too frail to make it through treatment or surgery. The woman before me was the most faithful woman I knew and the one who understood me, including the crazy spiritual gifts. She was the first person I told about the events with the messenger in Germany and the one who wrote me encouraging notes about my writing.

Don't give up. A note would come in the mail, unexpected, often when I received a rejection. *A diamond isn't noticed until it's found. Someone will take notice and see the gem in you.*

She understood me, and I knew I needed to let her go. My voice quivered. "Sweetgraw, why are you still here? I know you're ready to go and experience heaven. If you're tired, then I know God is ready."

Her voice was as strong and steady as I'd remembered it when I was a young girl. "Shannon, I have seventy-two descendants. You have two."

This simple statement hit me in the gut. Coming from a large family, I took for granted the impressive number of cousins, second cousins, and even third cousins who all came from Sweetgraw's children, my aunt and four uncles.

"I pray four rosaries a day for all of them. Do you know only a handful of you are still Catholic? And not many more of them are attending any kind of Christian church?"

Seeing her cry was like a dagger to my chest. "Sweet-graw, I know it is hard to see, but you also know you'll never live the day to see all of them come back to the Catholic Church. At this point, you can do more for them in heaven than you can here on earth."

The grip she had on my hand tightened so much, I swore I heard my bone crack. "Will you pray for them? Will you do this for me when I'm gone?"

The daunting task kicked my selfishness into high gear. "Oh, I don't know if I can do much better than you have, Sweetgraw. But I'll try. Of course I'll pray for them."

Realizing this could be the last time I'd see her on this earth, I felt the sudden need to ask for my own request. "Sweetgraw, when you're in heaven, please don't stop praying for me. You're the only one who really understands me, and I want to know you will always be with me."

"Always."

I leaned forward and kissed my grandmother for the last time.

One month later, I was in Arizona for a youth minster conference. I was restless and couldn't sleep, so I went for an early morning run. My spirit cried out in prayer as I ran. *All I want to do is reflect You, Lord. That's all I want to do. Save me from me.*

Save me from me. Save me from me. All I want to do is reflect You.

I prayed over and over again as sweat mingled with tears and stained my cheeks. On all accounts, I was in a good place, yet a truth deep inside remained covered. It bothered me, because whatever it was I knew, it kept me from believing in me. I had all the belief and trust in God. He had revealed His glory and majesty to me and within me, rerouting my prideful heart. I needed help with the unbelief that whatever was deep within me wouldn't surface and disappoint.

When I got back to the hotel, I was met by my sleepy roommate holding my cell phone in her hands.

"Neal's called you three times, and it's only 5:30 in the morning." She thrust the phone into my hands before shutting the door and presumably going back to bed.

My toes and fingers tingled with the anticipation of what news could be waiting for me this early in the morning. Good news rarely came with an early-morning call.

Neal answered on the first ring. "Shannon, where've you been?"

"I went for a run. I couldn't sleep. What's going on? Are the boys okay?"

"Yes, they're fine. It's Sweetgraw." He paused slightly but long enough for me to hear the catch in his breath. "She passed away an hour ago."

It wasn't surprising to hear. She told me she was ready. But having her actually gone took my breath away. I had the phone to my ear, and my other hand covered my trembling lips. I couldn't speak.

"Shannon?"

"I'm here." Barely. I wanted to hang up, climb into bed, and cry myself back to sleep.

"Your parents don't want you to leave yet. They have to wait on relatives to fly in, and so they'll probably wait till the end of the week to have the funeral."

The funeral. I recalled Matt's visitation at the funeral home. Walking up to his casket, seeing a pasty person who resembled Matt but had no spirit, no life, no joy. I remember almost believing it was a sick trick, until I saw his hands. He had this nervous habit of rubbing the edge of his pointer finger with his thumb. His hands weren't folded on his chest, nor did they lie flat. One hand was by his side, while the other was positioned as if he were rubbing his thumb and finger together.

I'll never forget it. It made my loss real.

I didn't want Sweetgraw to look fake. I knew she was gone, but the thought of seeing her without her spirit unleashed the sorrow. Neal stayed on the phone with me through it all until I was spent. The tears were a mixture of a selfish sadness and joy. I would not have the opportunity to see her, hug her, or hold her hand again, but now she was where she truly longed to be, dancing with Papa.

The second we hung up, I called the funeral home, which was owned by one of my dear high school friends. It was a family business, and I knew my friend, Charlie, would be the one taking care of my grandmother. All I had to do was tell the secretary who I was and he picked up the line.

"Hi, Shannon. You doing okay?"

"I'm okay. She's with you, isn't she?"

"Yes, she is."

My body eased. Charlie's family and mine went way back to our fathers' shared childhoods. Plus, Charlie knew me, and I knew he'd understand why I needed to ask him this favor. "Charlie, please make her look like herself. Don't overdo it or . . . " I couldn't finish.

"Shannon, you know, every time I would see your grandmother at events here in town, I always could see you in her. She was a beautiful lady, and I'll make sure she is as she always was—classy."

I smiled and giggled. That was Sweetgraw.

When I hung up with him, I sat down in the hallway and prayed a rosary for her.

The sun peeked above the horizon and shed natural light through the windows. It reminded me of the beauty my grandmother saw in the world.

An added blessing at this particular youth minister's conference was beginning with a one-day retreat. I was a second-year attendee, and those of us who'd been before got to spend the day in prayer.

My roommate was a first-year attendee, so she was obligated to go to all of the intro sessions, which meant I had the day to myself and no one needed to know my grief.

In the first prayer session of the day, Matt Maher, an unknown Christian musician at the time, led us into worship, saying, "Pray without a purpose. Sometimes we get caught up in how we pray or what we are going to pray, but this morning I want you to let the Holy Spirit guide you in your worship."

He strummed his guitar with his eyes closed, playing a soft ballad. The music poured out like a libation. All around me I heard others sing along. Some hummed, others whispered, "Come, Holy Spirit" and other soft utterances of love and devotion to God.

I closed my eyes and laid my head in my hands. The tears fell unseen to the ground. I felt as if I was amidst a chorus of angels, and I was comforted in being a part of the prayer without actively participating.

This lasted for nearly an hour of worship before Matt led it to an end. By then, my contacts were dry and I could tell my eyes were puffy and swollen. I walked out of the meeting room to use the restroom before the next session began, when a man, with a conference-attendee nametag, stopped me.

"Excuse me?" He reached out to touch my arm as I passed him on the way to the bathrooms.

"Yes?" I stopped but was embarrassed because I knew I probably looked like a mess after crying all morning.

"I . . . " He hesitated. "I have something I . . . " He stopped, and his face became crimson.

Why was he embarrassed? I looked down at myself to see if maybe I had a zipper open or a hole in my shorts. When I didn't see anything out of the ordinary, I looked at him again.

He was an unassuming man. Short, possibly an inch taller than me, with dark features and kind eyes.

"You're going to think this is crazy, but I have a message for you," he said.

My feet turned to cement cinder blocks. *Are you kidding me?* But something in his mannerisms put me at ease. He wasn't threatening, and we were two feet away from the conference room and surrounded by all of the attendees. The blood flowed through my veins and I could feel my feet again.

"Well, I don't think you're crazy," I said.

He gave me an odd look and pointed to a landscaping ledge that was still in the same vicinity as everyone but where we could have a private conversation. "Let's sit down."

The poor guy's hands shook, and he kept rubbing them on this legs.

"It's okay," I said. "I've had this happen before."

His head shot up and his eyes got wide. "Really? Because I'm thinking this is nuts, but I *know* I need to tell you these specific messages that came to me while we were in prayer."

I nodded. My heart pounded in anticipation.

He sighed. "Okay, I want to get it right." He bent over and put his head in his hands to think. After a second or two, he sat up. "Okay, I don't know what any of this means, but bear with me."

I nodded and smiled.

He looked me in the eyes. "I'm with you." Tears formed in his eyes.

The conviction of his voice made my heart speed up with hope, but I couldn't help but think it was too good to be true. He saw me crying, so he's assuming this will help. How could he know?

His head was already in his hands again before I could respond. "Let me see if I can get this straight." He sat up again, his eyes determined when he looked at me. "You look more like me now than ever before."

Wow. Why would he say that? How could he know what Charlie said to me?

"I don't know what that means to you, but hold on. There is one more, and I'm really not sure it makes sense at all." His eyes stayed transfixed on mine as he paused, as if to get the courage to say it aloud. "You *do* reflect me, and I am proud."

Oh, my dear God. I heard both my grandmother *and* God in the message. How could this man have known what I prayed to God that morning? There was no rational explanation.

Like a babbling fool, I tried to speak through the tears and explain about my grandmother and the prayer, but it felt like there was too much to tell and it came out in a garbled rush. I finally managed to thank him and explained I'd had this type of message given to me before.

"You are blessed, because I've never felt so strongly as I did this morning, knowing I needed to say something to someone I received in prayer." He held out his hand. "I'm Richard, by the way."

I shook his hand and thanked him a few times before I could tell he was the uncomfortable one.

When I didn't see him again that day, I worried it was all in my imagination, but thankfully I saw him with his group the next day, and he introduced me. "She is the one I had to give a message to."

There was no better gift than to have validation of God's promises, that He listens and we live life everlasting.

The next morning, I wrote in my journal:

June 13, 2006
5:41 a.m.

Lord, I am a witness to Your majestic canvas as I sit on this rock on what I would consider a mountain — others would probably call it a hill. The sun is barely edging into the horizon, offering a pale orange backdrop to the mountains before me. It is a beautiful sight. You are a beautiful sight. You promised I would see You in the sunrise, and I certainly am. You promise so much, and You always deliver.

Now it's changing to deep coppers and reds. A blanket of thick clouds hangs high enough above the horizon to give the sky a sense of protection. Lord, what I see most as the sun continues to edge up is the illumination as each minute passes. The sun broadens the horizon, shedding light on more of the world around me.

As I get to know You more and allow You to shed Your light on my path, I am given more understanding, wisdom, strength, and trust.

And all the lights in the city that seemed to take away from the brilliance of the sunrise now are so dim, they no longer hold a threat to the beauty of what lies before me, just as all the worldly things that threaten to keep me from Your light grow dim as I seek You more.

Thank You, Lord, for this awesome display of Your love and gift of beauty.

Yesterday was hard. I will miss Sweetgraw, and I'm selfishly sad because she was my support—the one who got me. I know she was tired and is happier with You. You never cease to amaze me, and I am grateful for Your generous message and love.

As I lay my grandmother to rest, help me to hear You, to reflect You, and to guide others in their journey of knowing You. Most importantly, help me to help my family so I don't let Sweetgraw down.

I'm blessed.

The following day was the end of the conference. Before I left for the airport, my father called to tell me that Sweetgraw, before she passed, planned her funeral and had chosen me to read one of the readings. Out of her seventy-two descendants, she chose *me*. It wasn't until he told me what I was reading that I might have understood why. She didn't choose a reading; she wanted me to *pick* what I felt was best.

Right? No pressure.

On the flight home I prayed for God to give me direction as to what could best serve our family in this time of loss and celebration of life. *"I've run the race"* came to mind.

I knew it was a passage often used at funerals, so when I got home I looked it up. What I found compelling and quite poignant was the passage that led up to the piece about running the race. It was 2 Timothy 4:1–5, and as I read it I could see my grandmother crying in her chair, begging me to pray for her family to come back to their faith.

Every family dynamic is different, and no one is immune to the enticements of the world. My grandmother had witnessed the struggle of many generations battling the worldly fight as the time passed in ninety-five years, with her family ravaged by drug and alcohol abuse, children born out of wedlock, divorces, homosexuality silenced by shame and fear, abuse, and greed. I could imagine Sweetgraw reading this to her family, and I knew it was divinely appointed:

> *I charge you in the presence of God and of Christ Jesus, who will judge the living and the dead, and by his appearing and his kingly power: proclaim the word; be persistent whether it is convenient or inconvenient; convince, reprimand, encourage through all patience and teaching. For the time will come when people will not tolerate sound doctrine but, following their own desires and insatiable curiosity, will accumulate teachers and will stop listening to the truth and will be diverted to myths. But you, be self-possessed in all circumstances; put up with hardship; perform the work of an evangelist; fulfill your ministry.*

This is the charge my grandmother, I believe, would have wanted to say to her family, had she had them all in front of her. By no means was Sweetgraw perfect. I've been told by my older cousins she grew to be a different grandmother than the one they knew as small children. Instead of making me think differently of her, this endeared me to her more, because it showed we are all weak and flawed. It is never too late to become the person we were created to become.

The passage goes on, in verses 6–7, to say:

For I am already being poured out like a libation, and the time of my departure is at hand. I have competed well; I have finished the race; I have kept the faith. From now on the crown of righteousness awaits me, which the Lord, the just judge, will award to me on that day, and not only to me, but to all who have longed for his appearance.

After the funeral, we gathered with family and friends for a reception honoring Jacqueline Frost McGraw (Sweetgraw). The story of the messenger coming up to me at the conference spread throughout the family like wildfire, and everyone wanted to hear it again and again. Cousins, aunts, and uncles complimented me on the reading and acknowledged how it spoke to them. I smiled, knowing Sweetgraw was looking down upon them with a great amount of love.

CHAPTER 17

MICHAEL

For God did not send his Son into the world to condemn the

world, but that the world might be saved through him.

John 3:17

Neal was as affected by my grandmother's death as I was. She was the one he chose to be his Confirmation sponsor as he entered the Catholic Church. He trusted what happened with the man who gave me the message. I believe it touched him and helped him believe what happened with the messenger in Germany. I'd imagine it's not easy for Neal to hear those stories, especially when I find them hard to accept myself and they happened to me.

Invigorated by faith, prayer, and my strengthened call to make more of my life, I found myself deeper into everything ministry. That summer, Neal joined me. He went to the Steubenville conference as a chaperone and witnessed firsthand what swept me off my feet.

Eight thousand teens packed the coliseum. It was an explosion of colored T-shirts from corner to corner. Hands clapped and girls squealed in delight while the boys remained cool. It wasn't until the host got the crowd going with skits and icebreakers that the boys gave in and participated in the song gestures.

It was a weekend of worship, adoration, and talks. I thought for sure this would be the time Neal and I would bond and grow together in ministry. We'd work with the teens together and grow closer in Christ as *one*. I wanted this for us and our family.

"I'm not singing or dancing. And I'm not doing hand gestures." Neal stood in the back of the group with his arms crossed. He smiled and kept time to the music by bobbing his head.

I'd look back every now and then, concerned the other boys in the group would follow suit. The boys were standing right next to him, *participating* in worship. They had their hands up, and at one point Neal put a hand on a young man's shoulder and bent over him in prayer.

On the last night of the conference, after the teens heard speaker after speaker discussing topics on morality and chastity and everything in between, the program went into adoration. The priest exposed the Blessed Sacrament, and the host and other speakers read from the Bible, encouraging teens to bring their fears, behaviors, and addictions in prayer.

My flesh was electrified with the presence of the Holy Spirit, and my heart ached for the teens in my group who were led to tears in prayer, desperate to embrace the love God poured upon them. I kept busy praying over every teen in my group. I knelt down beside them. "Just say Jesus." My priest taught me that was the best prayer to give when the teens were amidst the Spirit.

I looked up at Neal and saw him sitting on the edge near the group, with a young woman from the group. Mascara ran down her face, and her mouth was open wide. Neal put his arm around her and said something. She bent her head in prayer, and I saw him close his eyes and his lips move.

Thank you, God.

Neal tried, and I loved him for it, but I also knew this wasn't for him and that's where we differed. I loved everything about the charismatic culture of our faith, and Neal was more of an old-school traditional.

When I received a call that fall to be a speaker on the following summer's Steubenville conference team, I was elated. It was a dream come true—a dream I never knew I had. Had someone told me these amazing opportunities and spiritual blessings would occur in my life, I would have walked away, certain I'd met a crazy person who'd lost their mind.

God had shown up in my life. A new world was revealed to me with endless opportunities, all because I'd surrendered my life to God.

Thanksgiving Day that same year, a little over nine months since I'd received the emergency hysterectomy, I fell ill. My parents were in town, and I was preparing my contribution to the Thanksgiving meal that was to be served at my in-laws' home, and like a punch in the stomach I felt sick. There was no fever. I felt queasy. It was centralized in the middle of my stomach. I managed to get through cooking the meal and made it to my in-laws' home. I took a few antacids and settled down on the couch, thinking, *I'll lie here till it passes. It's a twenty-four-hour virus. No big deal.*

An hour passed, and the pain worsened. I didn't want to get the others sick, so I drove myself home a few short blocks away.

I had been home about ten minutes when the pain grew more intense and centralized in my side. Because of the surgery and complications from nine months prior, I realized it might be my appendix. I grabbed the phone and made it to the bathroom, only to fall on the floor, doubled over in stabbing pain.

"Neal." My breath came in rapid succession. "I think it's my appendix."

"I'm on my way."

Within seconds of hanging up the phone, I felt a blow to my stomach, as if someone had taken the end of a baseball bat and rammed it into my side. I don't recall much from this point except to open my eyes and see the tops of the trees whiz by as I lay in the passenger seat of my parents' car.

I have a vague recollection of nurses trying to straighten my body out enough to get a CT scan, but the pain was so intense, my body protected itself, remaining in a coiled position. I heard moans and cries, and at some point I realized they came from me.

Floating voices swirled around me.

"It could be an ovary."

"No, I think it's the appendix."

"It's all over the place. It's too hard to tell."

I was evening when I woke. My contact lenses were in, which was odd because I knew when I had my last surgery, I removed everything.

Dad and Neal flanked either side of my bed, and once they saw my eyes flutter open, they both hovered.

Neal reached down and kissed my forehead. "You doing okay?"

I nodded and tried to sit up, but the effort sent a wave of nausea and pain through my midsection.

"Hold on, now." Dad's voice was gruff. "Stay still. No need to move around."

"What happened?"

"Well," Neal said, rubbing my arm above where the IV was inserted. "Your appendix ruptured. It took them a while to get you cleaned up because you are septic. You'll have to be here until all of the poison is drained."

He pointed to my side.

Gingerly, I lifted up the covers and saw a plastic tube protruding from my side attached to what looked like a rubber lightbulb filled with blood and puss. My head spun. I dropped the sheet and lay back down. "That's disgusting."

"It is." Dad sat back down.

In the haze of medication, I dozed in and out of sleep as nurses entered my room to take vitals, check the bulb, and replace it with a new one. For two days the pain medication kept me in a fog, and finally by the third day I felt it fade.

Family and friends came in and out, kept me company, and watched sitcoms and Lifetime movies. My parents stayed in town an extra day and left after my fourth day in the hospital. I wasn't in any more danger, but I couldn't leave until all of the poison was gone or it would contaminate my other organs.

I was a grease pit. I couldn't take a shower because of the drainage tube, so I was left to do a one-handed sponge bath. My hair hadn't been washed in almost a week and was three shades darker than normal and stuck to my head like a helmet. I couldn't stand to look at myself, let alone have visitors come in and see me in this condition.

I waited for the nurse to check my vitals, then asked, "Would you mind helping me wash my hair?"

"You haven't had help washing your hair? I'm so sorry. You're so quiet in here. I guess we took advantage."

"Quiet?" It didn't make sense. What were they taking advantage of?

"Most patients get irritated and difficult after they've been in here for more than a day or two. You've been in here all week, and you're always smiling and polite. I guess we assumed you were fine."

It struck a chord. It wasn't the first time I would be "looked over" because I didn't feel worthy enough to make a stink or cause a commotion because I needed help. At the same time, I felt guilty for asking her to help wash my hair. I didn't want to be a nuisance like the other patients.

Instead of this visit being about me, I wanted to make it about them. They worked hard. They were in charge of my health, so I needed to make sure they were happy. Many wonderful conversations formed from this new exchange. I came to know my nurses and what shifts they held, what worried them, and what stresses waited for them at home.

By the sixth day, I felt like I'd become a main fixture on the hospital floor. The sepsis wasn't letting up, and it looked like I still had another two to three days of drainage before they would let me go home. It wasn't what I wanted to hear, but I felt a strange peace.

In the very early morning hour of four o'clock on the seventh day of my stay, a young African-American man came into my room. He had a fresh "out of graduate school" eagerness about him. He wore scrubs, so I figured he was a nurse I hadn't met, in to do the early-morning temperature and blood-pressure checks. I am a light sleeper, so when he walked in I opened my eyes and turned to face him.

He walked up to the bed and looked down at me. "I need you to tell me why I should believe in God."

God is my loving witness, and I'll never forget it. Like cold water poured over my head, I sat up wide awake. "Excuse me?"

"I've been hearing a lot about you, and I want to know why you believe in Him so much. Tell me why I should."

"It hasn't been easy," I said, "but God has shown me in ways that can't be doubted that He is real and that He has a purpose for me. I *need* to follow His will."

We went on with a conversation for an hour before he looked at the time and realized he needed to continue working. I never saw him again, and I never found out if he ended up believing in God.

These experiences solidified my faith even more and encouraged me to be bold with my truth. I wrote fervently to finish the book, took every opportunity to speak to other youth groups, and put everything I had into the youth group at my parish. My intentions were good, but all that work kept me from seeing my marriage falling to the wayside at home.

This time it wasn't so much about our sexual relationship than it was about not being on the same spiritual page. It wasn't a problem our marriage counselor could fix. One of us would have to step off our pedestal of pride and recognize we needed to bring our relationship directly into God's hands.

Leading retreats and speaking at conferences and every youth program took precedence over my family. The more Neal resented my time at church, the more I stayed away from home. When I was approached to attend a new parishwide retreat called ACTS, I jumped at the opportunity to once again get away from the discomfort at home. Plus, I wouldn't be in charge; this retreat would be for me.

I had an attitude going into the retreat, as well. The retreat aspect was what I needed, but by this point I had led so many retreats, it was hard for me to be led. It wasn't until I sat with my small-group table and listened to the speakers give their testimonies based on the different themes of ACTS (Adoration, Community, Theology, and Service) that I recognized how many other women struggled with the same issues I kept at bay.

When we discussed the talks among our small group, it opened my eyes to what I'd been missing over the past few years: adult conversation. From being at home with little kids to youth ministry, I was the one giving the advice, the mentoring, the love, and the correction, but I also needed to receive.

After one talk in particular, our group realized a sorrow we all shared but had never spoken about before: the loss of a child through miscarriage.

"I've had eight miscarriages." The young woman who sat next to me didn't flinch when she revealed her loss. Instinctively, I put a hand on her arm to console her.

She smiled. "I hate to say it, but when you keep trying and continue to miscarry, you become numb to the loss. Her story . . . " She stopped. Her hands went up to cover her face. "I'm sorry. I just never thought of these eight miscarriages as my *children*. We ended up adopting two beautiful kids."

I was shocked to hear this because I didn't realize her children were adopted. They looked like her and her husband. I couldn't fathom suffering what I had gone through once eight times.

"I've miscarried too." I spoke up because I knew she needed time to cry. "I had twins, but one 'vanished' and the other one survived—my son Ryan. There are times when I think about what it would have been like if both had survived. But it's too hard. I feel like I've felt him before, but I've not baptized or given him a name like she did with hers."

The ladies nodded, and some shared about their own experiences with miscarriages while the young woman next to me silently cried.

A woman across the table spoke up. "It's nice to think our babies are in heaven—probably not babies at all, but young men and women."

This shook me to the core. I had always felt I knew the child I lost was a boy. I had even felt him come to me when Ryan was about three years old. I was in bed with my eyes closed but not sleeping and felt a presence standing at my bedside. I assumed it was Ryan because we had moved him into a "big boy" bed, and he made a habit of getting up in the middle of the night, wanting water. But when I opened my eyes, I saw a brilliant white light the same height as Ryan but with no form. My heart pounded, and it felt as if it reached out to touch me, and that is when I cried out and turned on the light. After I tried to tell Neal what I'd seen and he had mumbled his disbelief, I turned off the light and realized who it could have been.

I begged for him to come back, but he didn't. There were moments when Ryan played in his room by himself and would laugh and talk as if someone was with him in the room. Again, I felt it could be his twin but I brushed it aside.

All of this happened, but I never thought to give him a name, though I knew in every part of me that the miscarried child was a boy.

I couldn't go any further with the retreat. My heart was stuck on giving the child a name and a blessing. Overstepping my place as a retreat attendee, I went to the director and my parish priest and gave him my idea.

"Can we do a blessing for the children we have all miscarried and lost?" My voice cracked. "Almost every woman at my table has suffered a miscarriage or more than one. I know there are more women in here who could benefit from doing this."

Apparently there *were* others in the group that needed the same closure as I did, because the director cut a part of the retreat that was more "fun time" and our priest held a blessing for all those who had lost children.

"For those of you who have lost a pregnancy due to any circumstance, if you will please come forward to receive a blessing," he said.

A breeze went by the nape of my neck, and my hair stood on end. I took a deep breath and walked up front. The young woman who suffered eight miscarriages came up and stood next to me.

There were eighty women at the retreat (including those attending and those serving on team), and many came forward.

The priest's face fell in sadness and understanding. I looked behind me and found only a handful of all the women present still in their seats.

It was heartbreaking.

The priest opened his book of blessings. "I want you to hold your hands in front of you, palms up. Now close your eyes and think about each pregnancy you've lost. Imagine your child. Son or daughter. And give him or her a name. If you've lost more than one, do this with each child."

I stood with my hands open to heaven and felt my son, Michael, come stand by my side. He felt to be the same height as my son Ryan but with a different, calmer spirit.

Michael.

God gave me his name. It was written on my heart. He had been with me and Ryan all along.

I heard children's laughter, I looked at the young woman who'd suffered through so many miscarriages and I knew she felt the same.

The priest took holy water and came up to each of us, making the sign of the cross on the palm of our hand with the water. "What is your child's name?"

My heart filled with pride. "Michael."

"May God bless the repose of Michael's spirit. In the name of the Father, the Son, and the Holy Spirit." He put a hand to my forehead and whispered a prayer. "May God bless you."

He went to the young woman next to me and she named off each and every child she'd lost. I could see the shock in the priest's eyes.

The smile on her face only showed joy.

When we all dispersed and had time to reflect and embrace the gift we'd been given, my friend came up and hugged me. "I felt them all. They were laughing, and I knew every one of their names."

"I heard them too."

We both laughed through our tears.

On the last day of the retreat we were given an opportunity to share what the retreat had done for us personally. I listened to one woman after another talk about her moment of finding God, feeling Him as I did a few years before on my own bedroom floor. It hit me, how high my pedestal had become and how I'd set my family aside. The truth was humiliating, but I knew I needed to share.

I stood up in front of the seventy-nine women. "This retreat has given me so many gifts that will change me for the better," I said. "But one thing I know is that I'm addicted to my job in youth ministry, and I've allowed it to come between my family. I know I need to look at my priorities and put my family first."

I sat down and rubbed the chill from my harms. I couldn't believe I'd said that out loud. My heart beat fast. God had redirected me once again. I couldn't wait to tell Neal.

When I came home from the retreat, I wanted to sit with Neal and tell him all about what I'd experienced and the revelations I received.

"Can't talk now," he said. "I'm meeting some guys at the club. We'll talk later."

He'd been home with the kids for four days. I couldn't blame him, but it solidified my knowledge of what I'd done. I'd allowed a new wedge to come between us.

CHAPTER 18

WORTHY

"However, you have a few people in Sardis who have not soiled

their garments; they will walk with me dressed in white,

because they are worthy."

Revelation 3:4

Neal couldn't care less about my experience on the ACTS retreat. I told him about naming our child Michael, and he was interested but the animosity was too deep. I had left him again with the kids. I left him alone all the time with the kids to do ministry work, and he wasn't happy.

We had regressed quicker than I could bat an eye. The way we spoke to each other was with a mutual disrespect. All I wanted was to be on the same page and have Neal be the man that would back me up in my ministry, maybe even be a part of the ministry *with* me, and to support me.

It didn't help how refreshing it was to meet more and more men within the world of youth ministry who displayed a complete belief and trust in God. These men prayed aloud, adored their wives, and brought others closer to Christ. They weren't skipping Mass because they didn't feel like going, and they understood the work of ministry was not a typical forty-hour workweek.

I loved Neal, and we weren't in such a bad place that I wanted to leave him or end things. On the contrary, I was desperate to share everything I was learning about our Catholic faith and my personal faith with him. I couldn't fathom the stress he was under with work and supporting a family. I wanted to pray with him so he could talk about these worries and concerns and be the one who would lead our family in prayer. I wanted him to be the head of the household, especially when it came to our family.

When I received the following letter from him, I knew I had to do something to help him—to help *us*:

Shannon,

For some reason I am feeling very melancholy. I've been doing a lot of thinking about life and what is truly important to me. I feel inadequate at times as a father and a husband. It's almost like I have not measured up, but I don't know what it is I'm supposed to gauge it against. Work and life can be hectic, so I try to escape to golf, but then I feel guilty with leaving you and the kids. For some reason I feel blah. I love you and the boys with all my heart and would give you the world if I could. I am not sure why I'm even telling you this, but I just feel lost. I try looking into my life to see what's missing, and I can't put my finger on one thing. I have a family, God, and friends, but I still feel somehow I'm lacking. If you have any suggestions, I'll take them. I love you and do not feel anything is wrong with our relationship. It's just I'm in a funk and overwhelmed with life. I pray to God every day to take control so I don't lose myself. I feel like a duck. On the surface all looks fine, but below the water my feet are going ninety miles an hour. I know everything will be fine, but I'm tired and maybe borderline depressed.

I love you,
Neal

"Why don't you go on the men's ACTS retreat?" I sat on the bed next to Neal, who flipped through channels on the TV.

"No."

"What? What do you mean, no? You need *something*. You said so yourself."

He looked at me with no expression on his face. "I don't need a retreat where I have to go and share my feelings with men. I don't sing. Besides, my prayer life is private."

I sighed. What he didn't know was I had signed him up anyway. A month before I went on my ACTS retreat, they had registration for the men's retreat. I signed him up as a surprise. I thought if I came back rejuvenated, he might reconsider.

When I got back from my retreat, his mood worsened. I called his friend, who happened to be on the men's retreat team.

"Hey, Neal still doesn't know I signed him up on that retreat, but I need to tell him," I said. "He's going to mad and do everything he can to find an excuse to get out of it."

"Don't you worry about it, Shannon. We'll work on him. We still have a few weeks."

"I told you I'm *not* going on a retreat. I don't need to pray with other people. I'm fine praying on my own."

"But you said you needed something that you were lacking. I *promise*—this retreat will help you figure it out. Besides, it's paid for and it would be good for you to get away from work for a few days."

"Get our money back. I'm not going. I can't take off work for two days."

"I already called your boss, and he supports you going on the retreat."

I held my breath for his reaction. I knew it was a bold step for me to take, but I knew he would use work as an excuse. His boss was a Christian man who agreed it would be beneficial for Neal to attend the retreat.

"You called my boss?"

"He said there was no reason for you not to go. That you have the time to take off and it'll be good for you. Really, what can it hurt, Neal?"

He stormed out of our room.

Lord, help us.

Two weeks before the men's ACTS retreat was my own
ACTS retreat reunion. Before the reunion, Neal and I had
to attend a meeting for a married couples' group at our
parish. The group was called Teams of Our Lady. It was
another push on my part to get us involved with other
Catholic married couples and introduce praying together
and with others.

Within the parish, this program had about twenty
groups, with six to seven couples in every group. Each group
had an RC—a "responsible couple"—who ran the meeting
for a year. This was our year to be responsible, which made
Neal that much more irritated.

"Why do we have to go to this meeting?"

"Because we're the RC and we have to meet with the
other RCs from the groups."

"Okay, but why do I have to go?"

"Because we are the responsible couple—not person.
It's not going to be long."

"And where are you going after the meeting? Why are
we taking two cars?"

"I've told you a thousand times, I have my ACTS reunion this afternoon and then I'll meet you at Mass."

"So I have the boys—again."

It wasn't a question. It was a statement. Loud and clear.

Begrudgingly, Neal followed me to the meeting. We
sat together on a couch, and before we began, while others
were talking and getting to know one another, the couple
leading the meeting asked me questions that pertained to

our parish. I worked at the parish, so they knew I would have more inside information.

I could not see Neal, but I felt his frustration. He shifted every few seconds on the couch and cleared his throat.

I couldn't concentrate on what they were asking because I was too preoccupied with Neal's frustration. I could almost read his mind: *You talk too much. You don't have to be the one that answers everything. You don't need to be the center of attention.* These comments were hurtful, and when he'd say them I'd get quiet, which was his point.

What is wrong with me answering questions about work?

The meeting began, and the couple asked all of us to answer a few questions about each of our teams and update them on a few things. They started on the opposite end of the circle, and we listened patiently until it was our turn. When it came time for us to speak, I decided to keep quiet and have Neal speak for us. He says I talk all the time, so I figured I'd let him speak. I knew he really didn't *want* to speak, but I wanted to make a point.

I sat back on the couch and looked to Neal to speak for us. Everyone in the room looked at us.

Neal turned to me. "You might as well speak. You'll talk over me anyway."

It felt like a verbal slap rang out in the silent room with a loud *snap!* My face burned with humiliation.

I giggled to diffuse the uncomfortable moment. "Ha, you're funny." I tapped his arm. "He just doesn't pay attention." I proceeded with the update of our team.

For the rest of the meeting, I fumed inside. *You might as well speak; you'll talk over me anyway* replayed in my head. I flip-flopped between the need to make everything seem fine and the strong desire to stick up for myself.

How dare you for embarrassing me! Who do you think you are? You can't treat me that way! My mind reeled with what I would say to him once the meeting was over.

The typical response would be for me to apologize and stuff what I felt inside. I surprised myself and headed straight for the door. I made it out without one word or glance his way.

In the car, on my way to the ACTS reunion, I gripped the steering wheel with both hands and screamed, "God, I can't do this anymore! If You want me to work for You and speak about faith, then I can't be a hypocrite with my marriage the way it is."

I should not have been driving, as the sobs wracked my body with each syllable spoken. "I want Neal to *support* me. I want him to *appreciate* me. I need Neal to *want* to pray with me. I want him to *respect* me and understand me. Lord, I can't change him! Only *You* can bring him closer to you. I can't do this anymore. You have to *do something*."

When I pulled up to the house for the reunion, I was a mess. I needed prayer, but I couldn't pray. I needed some of the women at the reunion to pray over me. What would they think of me? I don't want them to think bad of Neal. He's a good guy, but he can be a jerk!

I cried harder. I didn't want them to judge him or get the wrong impression. Neal was a good man and a good husband, but I needed *more*.

Despite the condition I was in, I walked through the front door, into the living room, and grabbed the first two women I saw. "Will you please come pray with me?" I asked them.

The look on my face must've told them I was desperate because they didn't question it and followed me into a nearby guest bedroom. I knew the owner of the home and therefore knew where we could go to have privacy.

I sat on the bed and faced the women, who were practically strangers. They were both on the retreat leadership team, so I knew they were at least well-versed in prayer through the preparation of the retreat. Other than the little bit I learned of them while on retreat, I barely knew these women.

They stared at me with wide eyes and looks of concern.

One spoke up. "Shannon, whatever you say here stays here. What's going on?"

Relieved, I poured out everything that took place that afternoon and Neal's personal struggle with stress and life. They already knew I realized my part in the mess, and I told them how I was already working on moving from full-time to part-time ministry in order to be there for the family. But I couldn't continue with a husband who wasn't willing to try and be on the same page in our faith.

"I need you to pray over me so I know what to do or say. I'm so upset right now, I can't think, so I need you both to pray."

"Oh, okay." They fidgeted.

Sensing a discomfort or a lack of experience in intercessory prayer, I grabbed both of their hands and held them. "Now, please, pray to God for me in this situation."

They squeezed my hands, and we sat in brief silence.

Finally, someone took the lead. "Heavenly Father, Your precious daughter, Shannon, needs You right now. Whatever it is that is going on within her marriage, we know You can make it right. We know we can do all things through Christ who gives us strength, and we are all here asking You to give Shannon the strength she needs to endure the issues in her marriage.

"Lord we all have issues in our lives that are hard to handle, but we know You give us the courage we need to push through. Please watch over Shannon and Neal and their family. Bring them together in Your name, and help them grow closer together with You. Let's ask Mary to pray."

Together we recited the Hail Mary: "Hail Mary, full of grace, the Lord is with you. Blessed are you among women, and blessed is the fruit of your womb, Jesus. Holy Mary, mother of God, pray for us sinners now and at the hour of our death. Amen."

My well was dry. The tears were gone, replaced with peace. These women both poured out their hearts for me, and I felt peace rest on my shoulders like a warm blanket.

When I came home that evening, I realized Neal had not gone to Mass. Frustrated at his indifference and still upset with the exchange earlier in the day, I went into the bedroom, where he was on the bed watching TV.

"Neal, I need to talk to you about today."

"Oh, you know you were going to talk over me. What I said was true."

I was furious that he seemed unaffected or apologetic about the event. "What? How . . . ?"

"You're nosy, and you want to be in everyone's business. You're always talking."

He attacked my character, which made me shut down. It was his sure way to make me stop.

I turned to walk away, defeated, when I felt a surge of courage and heard an internal whisper: *Don't give up.*

I stopped, took a deep breath, and turned back around. He sat on the edge of the bed.

"You said in the letter you have God and our family," I said. "You said you want God to take control so you don't lose yourself. Well, the way you acted toward me today was not you. In our relationship, it is supposed to be God and then us, together, as one." I used my hands to illustrate the point and clasped my hands together. "We are supposed to help bring one another closer to Him. But I'll be honest with you, what you did today hurt." I unclasped my hands and pointed a finger at him. "It felt like you were the *enemy* to me."

Neal sat on the edge of the bed with an expression of defeat, but he didn't say a word.

"I don't deserve to be treated like that, and from now on I will call you out when you put my character down again. I don't care if it is in front of your family, your friends, or even your co-workers. I don't talk to you like that and you shouldn't do it to me. You have four days before you go on this retreat." I paused to take a breath before I lost control of the tears pooling in my eyes. "I pray you find what you need there because this isn't right."

Neal never said a word about the exchange. We went about our typical schedule and spoke amicably to one another. He was reluctant to pack when it came time for him to attend the retreat send-off at the church. There was no way for him to get out of going. But he tried.

"I'm taking my own car to the retreat," he said.

"No, you're not. A bus takes you. *Everyone* goes on the bus."

"What if I need to leave? You know how my stomach gets."

My resolve remained. "You'll be fine."

I pulled up to the send-off and smiled at the obvious difference between the men and women's retreats. With the women's send-off, there were fewer cars because the men dropped them off at the curb and left instead of coming in to participate in the singing and hugging good-bye. But the parking lot was full at the men's send-off, and from the looks of long faces on the men, every wife had to drag her husband in by hand. If I'm not mistaken, I also believe some women stood by the doors to make sure no one escaped!

During the music and prayer, the men were stoic and unresponsive and the women were hopeful and desperate.

Essentially, we all wanted the same for our husbands: for them to feel freedom in Christ.

Not until I saw the red headlights of the bus did I breathe a sigh of relief. Thank God.

I prayed every day. I knew what he was experiencing and going through on every single aspect of the retreat, so I tailored my prayers to specific requests. *Help Neal relax. Give Neal the courage he needs to open up. Open Neal's heart to hear Your message of hope. Help Neal realize his worth.*

Plus the friend on the team texted me daily to let me know how he felt things were going. He told me who was at Neal's table, which was important because that would be who he would share with and hear about the most. When I found out he was with a young man who was on my core team in youth ministry, I flipped.

"I don't know if that's a good idea," I said. "He's way too charismatic for Neal. Neal will shut down."

The young man was one of my more charismatic and enthusiastic core members. He had a great testimony for being in his early twenties, but I also knew he was one who might rub Neal the wrong way.

"Shannon, don't you think God's got this?" my friend asked.

Oh, Lord, I pray You have this. He's right. I need to trust in You. Your plan is always best. You bring a greater good from everything. Help me to trust in You.

On Sunday, four days later, I attended the return Mass and reception. I patiently waited in the pews, with my boys flanked on either side of me, who watched for their daddy. The men processed in as a group, and I saw Neal stand next to the young man from my core team.

Well, at least he made it the entire weekend.

The men opened Mass with one of their gathering songs from the retreat. In awe, I watched as my husband put his arm around the young man and sang with his head held high.

Oh, my God. You are so good. I can't believe it.

All through Mass, I praised God in prayer. I could see the transformation all through Neal's body language and the genuine smile he gave when he sought us out as we sat in our pew.

At the reception I did my best to not ask questions. I wanted Neal to divulge what he wanted. He held on to my hand and introduced me and the boys to his new friends.

"This guy is the best." They'd slap Neal on the back and hug him.

"What a great guy. He's hilarious."

"You've got a good guy here."

I beamed with pride.

A man I'd known from working at the parish came up when Neal went to get the boys drinks. "Now he isn't just 'Shannon's husband.' He has a name."

I smiled, but inside his comment pinched. Did Neal feel like he was no one when it came to being here at the church? There wasn't time to dwell on it too much, as more and more men and their families came to meet us.

Finally when we found a break to sit down and eat, Neal looked at me with swollen, puffy eyes. "You can say it."

My cheeks burned. I knew what he was thinking, but I wasn't going to say anything. That wasn't the point. I shook my head in response.

"Oh, come on, I know you want to. Say it—'I told you so.'"

"No." I shook my head emphatically and smiled. "No, I don't want to say it. I'm glad to see you had a good experience, and I can't wait to hear about it—that's all."

On the car ride home, Neal held my hand as he told me about all the personal messages he received from hearing the speakers' testimonies and what he learned through the group at his table.

"We're going to pray together as a family," he said. "And you and I, we are going to pray together too. Every morning."

If he weren't holding on to my hand, I might have checked my pulse to see if I was still alive.

"You know that young man that volunteers for you?" he said. "He had the most influence on me this weekend. To be *that* young and know God the way he does is awesome. He said something that really resonated and changed how I look at life: 'It is my job as the husband to bring my wife and children closer to God.' He's right. It's *my* job."

My heart stopped. Was this really happening?

By the time we were in the house, tears welled up in Neal's eyes from recalling all the ways in which the retreat touched his heart. "I went to confession for the first time since we'd been married. *Eleven years.*"

He admitted he went to our parish priest, and I felt my knees get weak. In the past he'd get upset with me if I went to reconciliation with that priest because Neal felt like he didn't need to know our business because he was my boss. Neal had at least five priests from other parishes to choose from to confess to on the retreat, and he chose our parish priest. *Amazing.*

He stopped and looked at me real serious. "It was in confession I felt *worthy.*"

My breath caught. I reached out and hugged him because I knew how important that moment must have been. When he walked back into the bedroom, I looked up, held up a hand in praise, and mouthed, "Thank You, God."

Back in the bedroom, he showed me a few things he'd saved, and then he turned to me and gently held onto my arms as he looked me in the eye. "Shannon, if I have not been *supportive* of you and what God is calling you to and if I have not *appreciated* what you are doing or *respected* you the way you need me to, I am so sorry."

In one breath, I saw God through Neal and heard Him speak to me, giving everything I cried out to receive. My knees buckled.

Neal still had a grip on my arm. He held on to me, bent down, and wrapped his arms around me as I cried. He said,

"I know God is calling you to do something, and I believe in you. I'm always here for you."

CHAPTER 19
UNTIL DEATH DO US PART

Will you love and honor each other as man and

wife for the rest of your lives?

Catholic Rite of Marriage

True to his word, Neal and I prayed together every morning from that moment forward. Some mornings I rushed to get in the shower but knew he was about to leave for work, so in all the glory God gave me I'd sit with Neal on the bed, hold his hand, and pray. When his timing became *every* morning that I tried to get a shower in before handling the kids, I realized he got a kick out of this naked prayer.

Despite how I might have been dressed, prayer was awkward. Neal wasn't used to praying aloud, and I wasn't used to the intimacy prayer offered.

"Lord, please watch over the boys and Shannon as they go about their day," he'd pray. "Bless Shannon in the work You are calling her to do at the parish. And thank You for giving me the means to provide for my family."

Neal would squeeze my hand when he was done. I kept my eyes closed, afraid if I looked at him he'd let go of my hand and the prayer would be over. "Heavenly Father, I am grateful for our family and our marriage. Please keep us all healthy and safe from harm. Help me to follow Your will in my life. All I want to do is reflect You and help others see their worth in You."

I felt my face burn with embarrassment. "I am grateful for Neal and his job, for how he supports our family. Please continue to bless our marriage. Through Jesus Christ we pray."

And together we'd make the sign of the cross.

Our prayer was uncomfortable in the beginning yet peaceful. We were *meant* to pray together. My most intimate prayers *should* be shared with my husband. To hear him pray aloud for me and for God to bless me in ministry or for whatever retreat or talk I had coming up was a gift I never knew would feel so good.

The kids amused us in prayer. The boys were young, and though they were both used to praying with me at night and at school, now that Daddy led the prayer and made it more of a family affair in the living room, they took it more seriously.

Ryan would begin kneeling on his knees with his hands pressed together. "I pray for everything and everyone." As soon as he said it, he was up and bouncing from one end of the room to the next.

Seth mimicked Ryan. At times they surprised us and prayed for our dog, their babysitter, or someone in their class.

With God first in both our lives, we turned to Him together when times got rough. Or if one of us fell back into an old habit, it helped to see the lapse for what it was and to learn from it.

I stayed true to my promise and focused on family first over ministry and gave up working as a full-time youth minister and went into part-time young adult ministry. Because Neal supported me, I used my time wisely at home, and it seemed more opportunities came my way to speak publicly.

Life fell into place for Neal and me on many levels. Ryan, the year before the fourth grade, was taken off his medications by recommendation of his teacher and pediatrician. For a year he successfully continued to make straight As and showed personal restraint in some unacceptable social behaviors, like screaming when he'd speak. Ryan wanted to do well as much as we wanted him to succeed, and he showed us this with every passing year.

Opportunities opened up for Neal, and because of his loyalty, dedication, and work ethic he was known in his industry for his abilities. We recognized the compromise of both of us needing time together, time alone, and time as a family. We respected one another and gave each other the time and space needed. The animosity and frustration we used have because one felt the other "got more" vanished.

When the opportunity came to go on a work trip to San Diego, California, we jumped at the opportunity to get away on our own—to celebrate us for the first time in a long time.

The trip was picture perfect, with gorgeous blue skies during the day and a star-kissed sky at night. Neal played golf for "business" while I shopped with the other men's wives, and every evening we ate like celebrities. On the eve of our final day, we received texts from home telling us there was a possibility of a hurricane headed in the direction of the Gulf of Mexico.

Our kids were safe with Neal's parents. Neal had installed a generator that ran on natural gas in their home a few months before, but that didn't help calm our nerves. We turned on the TV to the Weather Channel to hear the latest, because California was only giving general updates on their local news channels.

I brushed my teeth, and Neal watched the TV like a hawk, waiting for the slightest bit of information.

"The hurricane is headed directly toward Galveston with a path right over Houston and Kingwood," he said. "Hurricane Ike."

"What? Are you sure? I thought it was headed more toward Corpus?"

Neal rubbed the back of his neck. "That's what it showed. Damn." He threw the remote onto the bed. "Do you know what that'll do to Kingwood, with all of the trees? The wind alone will knock out power, and who knows what our houses will look like when we get back."

"But we are so far out from Galveston. It'll lose strength, right?"

"That doesn't matter. It depends on how strong the winds are. I'm not worried about the rain, but those trees can fall and cut down power lines, cause fires, and destroy the houses."

Our entire group on the trip was from the same area, but we spent dinner doing our best to make the most of it.

"Maybe the storm will fade in the sea before making landfall."

"There's nothing we can do about it except pray."

It was the shortest dinner we'd had on the trip. No one was in the mood to carry on and enjoy any part of the evening. All we could do was wait and pray.

Neal paced the hotel room. I watched him rub his neck and back.

"You okay?" I asked.

"Yeah, it's just stress." He sat down in the desk chair.

"Do you want to pray with me?"

He had his hands clasped at his mouth. He nodded.

I patted the bed next to me. "Come to bed and we'll pray. You don't need to stay up all night."

He got up to join me. "I know Mom and Dad said the boys are sleeping, but I can't help but want to be there with them."

"I know, but there's nothing we can do."

We bent our heads in prayer and held on to each other. Neal nudged me. I knew he couldn't speak.

I prayed, "Lord, please watch over Ryan and Seth and Neal's mom and dad. Please keep them safe. We pray the storm will lose its strength and cause little or no damage. Help us to get home to our babies. And I pray for everyone with us, that all of our homes are safe from the storm. We ask this in Your name, amen."

The following morning, with only a few hours of restless sleep, we woke to hear the Weather Channel tell us about the obliteration Hurricane Ike caused on Galveston Island and Crystal Beach. We couldn't get a text to go through to Neal's parents and were informed by the news that power was out in thousands of homes in Kingwood, all the way to Conroe, Texas, an hour north of Kingwood. Airports were shut down. We couldn't get home.

Neal got on the phone and tried to reach anyone he could through his company to find out any information. After a few hours we managed to get through to his parents and found out they were all okay. The generator worked, so they had power in 75 percent of the house, including all appliances and AC units.

Neal's dad sounded amazed. "Your boys slept through it all. I can't believe it. Trees were falling all around us and wind shook the windowpanes. It sounded like we were in a war zone."

"I'm going to do whatever I can to figure out a way for Shannon and I to get home," Neal said. "We might have to fly into Dallas, but I'm not staying here."

Neal worked with the others to find another route home. Occasionally I saw him rub his neck, arm, and leg. It was obvious as the stress took its toll.

"Power is going to be out for at least a week, if not more, in Kingwood." Neal rubbed his neck. "I think I found a flight into Dallas, and I've talked to Dad. He and mom are going to drive the boys up to Dallas and meet us at the airport. Your dad is going to meet us in Dallas and take you and the boys back home to stay with him."

"What? Why?"

"Because from what Dad says, it's crazy in Kingwood. There's no electricity. It's hot, Shannon. Besides, food will go bad fast."

"If there are so many trees down, how are your parents driving out of Kingwood?"

"Dad said he saw a truck paving a way from their neighborhood to the highway. He's fine if he can get to the highway."

It was a blessing that his parents lived in the front of Kingwood, near the highway.

"What are you going to do?"

"I'm driving back with my parents. I need to see what damage has been done to our house, and work's already called. We need to get generators in to the customers."

I hated being without Neal at my parents', but I knew he was right. Being with two small boys and no electricity didn't sound fun.

Neal called the morning after he'd arrived home. "You should see this place. It's eerie. No lights are on, and massive tree trunks are laying all over the roads. You can't drive at night because there's no clear path."

"But no damage to our house?"

"No, none. The trees that could've fallen on the house are either still standing or went in the opposite direction. But you should see some of the houses from the main road. There definitely is damage."

"What's that loud noise? I can barely hear you."

"That's the generator. Can you believe our neighbor told me to cut it off last night? He's nuts."

Two days after Neal arrived home, he called late at night. "I'm not feeling right. I think I'm going to take myself to the ER."

"What? No one's going with you? Are you okay to drive? What are you feeling?"

It's a heart attack, I bet.

"Chill out. It's nothing. My right side feels funny. Not my left. It's like it's going numb."

"Oh my gosh. Seriously? Neal! Then go. Go *now*."

Five hours away from home, at the northern tip of Texas, I paced until I got word from Neal it wasn't a heart attack. They didn't find anything and sent him home.

Like a caged animal, I went crazy not able to know what was going on with Neal and our home. I convinced Neal and my parents I was fine to drive the kids home. I took one of Dad's work cars and settled in for the long trip.

Driving into Kingwood was like driving into a war zone. Massive tree trunks riddled the roads like candy sprinkles on a cupcake. There was so much cleanup and so much work to be done that even a week after the storm, it still looked like the storm just hit.

With precision and care, I maneuvered the car through the debris. I was shocked to find our driveway clear.

Thank you, Lord, for getting us home safe.

That night, Neal woke up in the middle of the night. "My shoulder is killing me and I can't feel my right side."

Oh no.

"Okay, let me call your dad," I said. "I'm going with you to the ER."

We sat in the ER for three hours among crying babies and men and women of all ages who looked as tired as I knew we did.

"If they don't see me in the next half hour, I'm going home." Neal held on to his shoulder, kneading his hand into the muscle.

"No, you're not."

An hour later, Neal was called back for some tests. A half hour later, they brought us into the a triage room.

"We are not finding anything out of the ordinary on your EKG, and your blood tests are normal. Your blood pressure is in normal range. You are not having a heart attack."

"What is it, then?" If it wasn't a heart attack then they needed to have some answer.

"It's been a stressful time for everyone."

"Yeah, okay." Neal got up in a rush. "I get it. This is from stress, right?"

The doctor put up his hands.

"Whatever." Neal pushed past me and out of the room.

"Thank you," I said.

I left and followed Neal.

A few nights later, Neal stumbled and fell into the wall. I could tell his gait was a bit off, almost like he was tipsy. He hadn't been drinking. He was just tired and stressed.

"Shannon."

I woke to Neal shaking me.

"Something's wrong. I don't care what that doctor said. This is *not* stress. I'm going to the minor emergency."

"You don't want me to go with you?"

"No. I'll be fine. I'll call you." He kissed me on the cheek and left.

Third time wasn't the charm. His blood pressure was high enough that the minor ER sent him to the hospital in an ambulance. Again, nothing showed up on his EKG, and even though Neal insisted he felt numb and couldn't walk well, they didn't suggest any other tests.

The next morning, I wouldn't let Neal leave the house. "Go to a regular doctor. Get them to take X-rays or an MRI, because this isn't like you to go to the emergency room three times in a row."

Neal called and got in with his general doctor, who took an X-ray of his neck, where he saw a slight hole that caused alarm. Once again I headed to the hospital, this time with a packed bag and a pounding heart.

When I got to his room, they prepared Neal for an MRI and spinal tap. Due to the symptoms of numbness on his right side and weakness on his left, combined with the apparent hole in his spine near the nape of his neck, they wanted to check out all possibilities.

Amidst the chaos of no power in the majority of homes in Kingwood, our friends stepped in like family. They took care of our children, brought us food, and prayed with us.

I sat on the hospital bed with Neal and held his hand when the doctor came in to give the prognosis.

"We are pretty certain you have transverse myelitis," he said, "which is an inflammation of the spine that could be causing the numbness on your right side. However, there are three lesions on your spine as well, so I want to do an MRI of your brain. If it is the transverse myelitis, it might go away within a month or two or take up to a year. The hole in your spine at the base of your neck is called syrinx. It isn't life threatening, and you have most likely had it all of your life. But I want to do the MRI of your entire brain so we can get a better idea of what is going on."

Before we could take in the information, two men came in and wheeled Neal away again.

This time when the doctor came back to deliver the results, my in-laws were in the room with Neal. I arrived from dropping the boys off at school. I stood at the door, thankful to see I hadn't missed the doctor's visit.

"We need to do a few more conclusive tests with the spinal tap fluid we took yesterday," he said, "but from the MRIs, we see you have lesions on the brain and the three on the spine. It isn't definitive until we get the final results, but it looks to be multiple sclerosis."

Multiple sclerosis?

The doctor did his best to explain, but at the time it didn't sink in. They gave Neal IV steroids for five days in the hospital. During this time, we researched more about multiple sclerosis online, which didn't help our outlook.

Multiple sclerosis is when the myelin sheath that covers the nerves in the brain and the spine deteriorates and causes a tear, or lesion, essentially making that nerve useless. The threat of MS is when the nerves are exposed or become useless and whatever area within the body the nerves control is affected. The area of the brain that gave Neal feeling on his right side was affected, which caused him to be numb from his chest down to his foot.

I lay beside Neal in the hospital bed and listened to him explain what he felt.

"It's like when your leg goes to sleep and you try to walk on it. You can't feel it, but you feel pressure if touched."

I ran my fingernails lightly along his thigh. "Can you feel this?"

"No. I know you're doing it, because I see you. I can only feel the pressure."

I moved my hand and buried my face into his chest so he couldn't see me cry.

Desperate to battle the disease, regardless of its history of having no known cure, we sought out the best. We managed to get an appointment with a renowned MS doctor in Houston at UTMB, who happened to also be the country singer Clay Walker's MS doctor.

Neal and I stood in the elevator in silence. The doors opened into a waiting room filled with debilitated men and women and their caregivers. Some with walkers leaned against their seats, others had walkers in their hands, and a few were in wheelchairs. Neal grabbed my hand as we took a seat. It wasn't a sight we expected, and it forced us to face his impending future head-on.

In many ways it reminded me of the moment I walked into the rheumatoid arthritis doctor's office and saw all of the artificial joints on display. I was officially in remission now but couldn't help picture Neal and me sitting side by side on our motorized scooters. I smiled at the thought. Humor is how I dealt with the uncomfortable, and it didn't hurt to imagine Neal and I drag -racing down a hallway on our pimped-out scooters.

By the time we were called back into the doctor's office, the lump in my throat was so wide I felt like I couldn't get any air. I was determined to be strong for Neal and not cry. He looked like he was in shock. I couldn't break down.

The doctor was eccentric, never quite looking either one of us in the eye. He talked fast and seemed a bit enthusiastic when he learned Neal had the Dawson Fingers (more than nine lesions on his brain), three lesions on his spine and syrinx (the hole in his spine near the neck). After a twenty-minute session that felt as if Neal was on an interview, the doctor broke down his options.

"You have relapsing-remitting multiple sclerosis. The fact that you have the Dawson fingers tells me you've had MS for a while without major symptoms."

I couldn't keep quiet. "Why did it show up now?"

"Usually stress is the catalyst to a flare-up."

Neal and I looked at each other.

"You can take either an interferon-based protein, like Betaseron—it comes in a pill form but is harsher on your stomach and liver—or a glatiramer acetate-base protein, like Copaxone, which is a daily injection. Both work well to keep you from flaring up, but there is no guarantee for the long term. Each person with MS is different. You can go without another flare-up for ten or twenty years and then immediately go into the secondary-progressive or progressive-relapsing phase. Or you can continue to flare up despite the medication and enter into the progressive phase within a few years."

Neal and I stared at him and blinked. It was like we heard him play the "Would You Rather?" game. Would you rather take a daily injection and *eventually* you'll be crippled, or would you rather take a pill and be crippled? Either way, both options sucked.

"There is no cure," he continued, "but we are working diligently to figure out the progression of this disease. Because you haven't entered into the secondary-progressive phase, you are a prime candidate for our research study."

Neal's eyes caught mine and he rubbed his eyebrow, a telltale sign he was nervous.

The doctor left the room.

"I'm not doing the study," Neal said. "I'm not taking the chance of being the one who gets a placebo and then ends up in his waiting room with a cane next year. Dr. Nguyen gave us the same treatment options. I'd rather just stick with him."

The doctor came back in the room. "Here is some information on both types of medication. And here is packet giving you more details on the research study."

We were out of the office building in minutes.

"You drive." Neal handed me the keys, which was another sign of his stress level. Neal didn't like my driving. I knew he needed his moment.

I prayed, *God, please give Neal the strength he needs right now.* It'd been two weeks since he'd been in the hospital and only a few days since he'd received the spinal-tap confirmation of the disease. There were moments Neal would sit and stare into space and rub his eyebrows. I'd make sure the boys, who were now old enough to understand Dad needed time to think, were quiet and out of his way. I waited for the moment he'd explode in anger.

Neal sat silent in the passenger seat. "This sucks."

I expected a few other choice words to express his pent-up emotions. I expected him to go into a rant and feel sorry for himself and complain about what he stood to lose because of this disease.

"You know, it is what it is," he said. The pain, thought absent in his speech, was evident in his eyes. "There is nothing I can do except take the medication the doctor suggests and continue to live life."

I was in awe.

Before choosing his medication, Neal took advantage of speaking to other MS patients and discussed his fears and concerns. He talked about it, and I listened. I waited for him to have a meltdown, to get angry and upset, but he remained calm—stressed, but calm.

For the next few months, he suffered through two more flare-ups that put him back on steroids. Steroid treatment is the hardest part of having MS because the steroid is the only drug that can stop the damage of the flare-up (when a lesion is considered active and damages the nerve, therefore debilitating the area of the nerve); however, the steroid altered his mood.

In the beginning, there were moments I felt I'd lost Neal completely. On the steroid, he wasn't the calm, rational man I loved. Instead he was volatile and on edge.

"Get out of my face!" he'd yell.

The look in Neal's eyes was evil. There was no trace of the calm and collected man.

I wanted to react and respond with my own anger, and it took every ounce of control to not slap him. I *knew* it was the medication because he wasn't making sense and he wasn't himself.

One day I took Ryan to Seth's baseball game. I sat alone at the top of the bleachers while Ryan played in the park and Seth was on the field. I allowed the tears to flow.

How am I going to get through the rest of our life with him like this?

I realized how often Neal might have prayed the very same prayer in regard to dealing with the many irrational blowups I had early in our marriage, not because of steroids but because of pent-up hostility and anger left as residual effects of the abuse.

Worse, family prayer became urgent pleas from the boys. "Help Dad get better, and make him happy again."

Neal winced as if he were stuck within this body, unable to be free.

One day I found Neal sitting on the edge of the bed with his head in his hands, crying.

"I don't mean to be this way," he said. "I'm filled with this rage and anger and I'm on edge and I don't know how to stop it."

Thankfully, the steroids were only a two-week ordeal. I went with Neal to his follow-up neurology visit.

"I think the next time he has a flare-up, we need to put him in the hospital," I told the doctor. "He rages, and I'm afraid he'll hurt one of us."

Neal reached over and squeezed my hand.

"I hate to say it, and I'm not exaggerating," I continued. "That, or he needs to live with his parents while he's on the steroids."

The doctor's eyebrows peaked. "I have a better idea. When I put him on the pill form of the steroids, they have to give it to him in higher dosage to enter into his system. But if we do an IV steroid, it is more mild but with the same results. A nurse can come to the house and put in an IV port and show you how to administer the medicine yourself."

Six months later, Neal had another flare-up, the third in his first year of diagnosis. This time a nurse came and put in an IV port. We all knew what to expect, and the boys and I gave Neal his space. Neal, too, was able to tell when the medication began to make him irritable, so he warned me, "It's starting, so if I say anything, know I don't mean it."

Living on edge is not living, but thankfully the daily IV medication took effect, slowed down the progression, and kept him tolerable. Taking advantage of the time we had, I did fewer retreats to free up more weekends to travel with him.

Our perspective on marriage and life in general changed drastically. The little things didn't matter anymore, not when he was faced with a disease that was incurable with the possibility of becoming blind, deaf, and physically handicapped, even to the point of losing the ability to swallow. Not one case we heard about multiple sclerosis was the same. It was a crapshoot. Neal could spiral down the rabbit hole and progressively get worse within five years or he could manage to go as far as twenty to thirty years without experiencing even one of the side effects.

He could die in a tragic accident before dying from MS, but the realization of the higher possibility of an impending doom forced us both to appreciate life day by day.

Carpe diem.

Living this way not only opened our eyes to the full beauty of what God had blessed us with in family and friends, but in the friendship we had with one another. I wanted to make sure we had moments and memories.

One of the first trips Neal wanted to take was to Rome. I planned a trip through the parish with our priest. Neal had never been overseas, and he wanted to see the Vatican and feast his eyes upon the history and all Italy had to offer.

We were blessed to have our priest with us and to celebrate Mass in many of the famous churches in Rome, including at St. Peter's, down below in the crypt of the Vatican, around the corner from Blessed Pope John Paul II's tomb. The most memorable was when we went to St. Clements, the site of the very first church, where the first Christians met in homes to celebrate the sacrament of the Eucharist. Over hundreds of years they had built another church on top of the original home, and then on top of that church they built St. Clements. It was here our priest offered to do a renewal of marriage vows for all married couples on the trip.

Neal and I locked hands and looked at one another, dressed in jeans and sweaters, with no fancy dress or professional hair and makeup. Just us. Simple. My heart pounded as I looked into my husband's eyes and I realized how much I wanted to say those vows again, this time paying attention to every word I committed to him without doubt or fear.

"I, Shannon, take you, Neal, for my lawful husband, to have and to hold, from this day forward, for better, for worse, for richer, for poorer, in sickness and in health."

My voice caught, and I realized I didn't have to vow it. *I lived it and I meant it.*

"Until death do us part."

EPILOGUE
FORGIVENESS

But now, thus says the LORD, who created you, Jacob, and formed you, Israel: Do not fear, for I have redeemed you; I have called you by name: you are mine.

Isaiah 43:1

As a survivor of abuse, I've learned the forgiveness I give is for me and not necessarily for the person or persons who harmed me. Forgiving is an act of letting go of the control the person or the act the person has afflicted and giving it to God, placing it in His hands and trusting He will take care of the person or persons as He deems suitable.

Sounds good in theory, but it isn't easy. I spent years in therapy in the beginning of my marriage to find a place to forgive the men who raped me and to forgive my grandfather for what he'd done to my mother and my sister. It took longer to work on the forgiveness of my grandfather and grandmother (because she knew the abuse was taking place and didn't do anything to stop it).

Once I'd come to a place of complete transformation with God, I knew holding on to anger and resentment poisoned me and not them. With pity in my heart, for I knew well that evil would reside in them if they didn't personally come to their own spiritual transformation, I placed them in God's hands.

What helped to heal was helping others, to have a voice and lead other survivors to find their voices.

But I was incomplete. As God led me into youth ministry and later into speaking, I found I felt more insecure with each accomplishment. I thought, *I'm not good enough.* My thoughts taunted me when I prepared for programs, retreats, and conferences. I'd journal and pray to understand what was hidden so deep inside, I couldn't quite overcome it.

Others who were older, wiser, and spiritually led gave me encouraging notes and made references to how obvious it was I needed to go deeper spiritually. Something kept me at the surface, and I needed to allow myself to sink below the depths of comfort to recognize what it was in order to overcome the insecurity.

In writing this book with Neal, I still struggled with the underlying nagging feeling there was a piece missing in my life that would make some of my behaviors make sense. I knew the rapes accounted for a lot of what I dealt with sexually, but there were other behaviors that didn't add up to what I'd gone through. In writing my previous book, *Exposed*, I had the same nagging feeling but quickly attributed it to what I'd endured as a child consuming my sister's behaviors.

I didn't want to dwell further on that dynamic of our family at the time, so I let it be addressed, acknowledged, and swept away because it was *their* story, not mine—until I came to write in this book about the counseling I received to embrace forgiveness. At the time, the logical need was to learn to forgive myself. Much was accomplished at the time, but even still, now eight years later, the underlying nagging feeling remained: *I'm not good enough.*

This is hard to admit when I speak to thousands on their self-worth, self-respect, and dignity. I *believe* God. I *trust* God. I know His love and that there is purpose planned for my life. But still I felt unworthy.

As I wrote about the time I was hypnotized and went to the young girl within me who needed me the most, I remembered going to a very young self, three or four years old— much younger than the age I'd been when I experienced anything tragic or witnessed my sister in her own demise.

Why had I not gone to a teenage version of me? But I put the thought away. When I wrote this memory, it was like taking a key and unlocking a treasure chest that had been lost in the depths of the sea for thousands of years. Once opened and the contents were revealed, they poured out and overflowed as if the chest were so old and brittle, it disintegrated and could no longer hold its contents.

The sounds, smells, flashes of memories, comments, words, and—worse—the feelings poured over me and fit like the last missing puzzle piece.

I was complete.

I, too, was molested by my grandfather.

The pain erupted, deep and searing. I could not stand to keep it in. In the sanctity of my home, I wailed and wept. It made sense. It all made sense. I rejoiced in the pain because *I finally made sense.* I had flirted with the knowledge this was my truth as well, but something always held me back from accepting I'd suffered the same abuse as my mother and sister.

Timing is everything, and I do believe when my spirit was ready God brought me to it because He knew I'd go through this with Him.

This truth helped me to understand some of my actions as a teenager that led me into situations that weren't smart or safe. I understood why I often had things done to me and yet I felt as if I were the one at fault.

When radio interviewers asked, "Didn't you have a good relationship with your father?" I'd be bothered by the question because I love my father and have a good relationship with him. I couldn't rationalize why I was desperate to feel love and sought love in situations that were clearly harmful.

I matter.

All I ever wanted to feel was that I mattered. Everything I fought for, everything Neal and I argued over, and all I reacted and responded to—it all came down to the little girl within me trying to say, "I matter!"

What my grandfather did to me does not define me. However, the knowledge of what was done helps to work on redirecting my thoughts to finally accept I *am* good enough and to believe it as much as I believe in God.

My grandfather passed away four months after my memories came back. I didn't have the opportunity to confront him, but in the end I knew I wouldn't have received the response I felt I deserved. It was best to put my grandfather in God's hands.

But I needed closure.

I feel righteous anger, pain, and betrayal. I couldn't understand why, but I needed to take the journey to be at his memorial service—not to celebrate his life but to give a voice to the little girl inside of me who needed to be heard.

His four sons stood before the handful of church friends and fellow veterans telling stories of their childhood together. I sat in the back and kept to myself, recognizing the difficulty of the task my uncles had in reconciling the monster I knew with the father who taught them the importance of loop traveling to see the most on a journey and how to take care of their lawns.

At the end of the day, alone in the chapel while everyone else was with his ashes, giving him a military salute, I came face to face with his picture.

"You hurt me," I said. I stood stoic, but the little girl came forward, shedding the tears.

"What you did scarred me and warped my security." The teenage girl emerged, outraged at the innocence he stole.

"I was too afraid to love, to get close, or to feel." I stood before his picture as a wife and mother and wept.

As angry as I was, I turned and walked away and gave myself the gift of letting go.

God is in control in the matter of his soul.

The forgiveness is for me, and right now I am still on my journey of learning to love the way God calls us to. I believe every person, no matter what evil he or she has done in life, is a child of God and deserves the same redemption as me.

What I am thankful for in surviving this journey is that God took the gifts He's given me from the moment of conception, along with the strength and courage I've received from the trials, to bring forth healing to all those who've been through similar pain.

God is relentless in finding a way to get us where we need to be. The journey of my life has clearly headed in the direction of helping others. The most recent endeavor is founding Hopeful Hearts Ministry, a 501(c)(3) nonprofit dedicated to restoring the lives of those who have been abused and giving them a voice.

I thank God for my life. All of it. And I thank Him for giving me a husband who was willing to give his life over to God and receive his redemption in full in order to lead me closer to Him. This is what forgiveness can bring: an appreciation of life and the freedom to embrace redemption.

ACKNOWLEDGMENTS

My deepest and sincerest gratitude goes to my husband, Neal, for joining with me in this endeavor, allowing me to put our marriage in such a vulnerable light to be examined, scrutinized, and hopefully used as an example of one of the greatest sacraments he and I could ever partake in.

Many thanks to Jenny Tomotaki, who patiently gave of her time and talent in the beginning drafts of editing, and to Nicole O'Dell for her willingness to share in her vast knowledge of the creative process, for seeing this book's potential, and for encouraging me not to let it go.

To Diane Morrow, Tina Jacobson, and Rick Roberson of The Barnabas Agency for believing this Catholic girl could reach across denominations and get to the heart of every Christian. Diane, you have championed me through many of life's trials as you struggled through your own, which has taught me a great deal about perseverance and fortitude. Thank you, thank you, thank you.

To Msgr. Chester Borski, Fr. Gavin Vaverik, Fr. Richard Barker, Fr. Ken Heberlein, Susan Synan LPC, and all of the priests and professionals who have helped Neal and me stay the course through our twenty-year marriage—I am indebted and grateful.

My endless gratitude goes to our fantastic friends and family, especially to those who helped us most recently in trying times: Kathy and Norman Deitz, Tim and Judy McGraw, Angela and Trey Whitley, Dan and Lauri Pradel, Guy and Terri Braden, Bo and Amanda McCall, Patrick Diamond, Clarissa Distefano, Jennifer Moore, Jenn and Mitch Karp, Sean and Jodi Diamond, Kent and Kerry Daigre, Chris and Michelle Pozzi, John and Stephanie Martinez, Mike Hales, Heather and Michelle Owen, Alicia Autry, Angie Glancy, Amy Banmiller, Rob and Tiffany Duncan, and Nora and Pat Twoy. You all have stuck by Neal and me, even when you wanted to push either one of us (or both) off the ledge. You have been a great support, encouragement, or example at some point in our marriage.

Finally, to my sons, Neal Ryan Deitz II and Seth Thomas Deitz, who had to endure the brunt of our mistakes. If I could rewrite our history, I would have not taken so long to stop the yelling, put away the selfishness, or embrace the gift we'd been given by God with both arms. You two have endured our pettiness and at the same time received our greatest love. Thank you for the prayers and being you—the greatest blessing in our marriage.

For all of the names I've failed to include, whether you are family, friends, supporters of Hopeful Hearts Ministry, or a random stranger who endured my need to talk, I want you to know you are *not* forgotten—thank you.

ABOUT THE AUTHOR

Shannon M. Deitz is the author of *EXPOSED*: *Inexcusable Me...Irreplaceable Him* and founder of Hopeful Hearts Ministry, an advocacy non-profit organization (501 c3) giving a VOICE to survivors of abuse. Shannon has spoken across the United States and in Sydney, Australia and Madrid, Spain addressing the realities and affects of abuse in our culture and the graces faith provides for one's healing journey. She is the spokesperson for the Maria Goretti Network (abuse survivor support group), has been a featured columnist with Choose-Now Ministries.com "Shannon Deitz: On Hope", featured on CatholicLane.com, Lifestyle & Charity magazine and Catholic Women's magazine. She and her husband, Neal, live in Kingwood, Texas, where they are active in their local church and community. The couple has two sons, Ryan and Seth, who provide them with endless joy and reason to continually count their blessings.

www.HopefulHeartsMinistry.com

CPSIA information can be obtained
at www.ICGtesting.com
Printed in the USA
LVHW09s1307130818
586823LV00001B/40/P